Making the Tough Call: Medical & Health Professionals

Making the Tough Call:
Medical & Health Professionals

Resource for Professional Reporters of Suspected Child Maltreatment

Kathryn S. Krase

Krase Consulting, Brooklyn, NY

CONTENTS

Parenting is NOT Easy

When I started training mandated reporters of suspected child maltreatment, I was already a lawyer, a social worker, an educator, and a researcher; I was not yet a parent. Before I was a mother, I trained mandated reporters based on the law and my experience with families in my professional practice. Over the past 15 years, as I've grown in my role as mother to my son, Jack, I have adjusted my orientation. I still train on the law and my experience with families in my professional practice, but now I bring personal lived experience to share and learn from as well.

The main take-away I offer from my personal and professional experiences is that parenting is NOT easy, even if you have the best child ever (like I do). Parenting is hard. Parenting is nothing like you ever imagined it could be and much more than you ever dreamed. Parenting is not for everyone. Some people love it, and some don't, but we are all parents, doing the best we can.

You might expect this book to be dedicated to the protection of children, but, instead, I dedicate this book to parents. No one would be here without parents in some form or another. Ultimately, if we want children to live long, healthy, and happy lives, parents, of all kinds, need the respect, attention, and support they deserve to make that goal a reality.

Introduction

Thank You!

Thank you for choosing to prepare yourself as best you can for your role as a professional reporter of suspected child maltreatment by picking up this book. This book is geared for medical and healthcare professionals who are required by the law in their state to report suspicions of child maltreatment; these professionals are usually called "mandated reporters." You may be required to read this book for your professional education program or have selected a related training to earn continuing education credits towards licensing requirements. Maybe, you just have a keen interest in exploring what a "mandated reporter" really means and want to think more about your obligations in that role. No matter what the reason you are reading this book, I commend you on taking this step to inform yourself; the role of a mandated reporter can be confusing and complicated. Hopefully, the shared goal of all who pick up this book is to protect children from harm and help families thrive. The more knowledge you can acquire and the more opportunities you can provide yourself to consider the implications of your role as a mandated reporter, the better for the children and families you are committed to serving through your professional service.

Who Am I

My name is Kathryn Krase. I'm a lawyer, a social worker, an educator, a researcher, and an expert on the reporting of suspected child maltreatment. Over the past 20 years, I have trained thousands of professional reporters of suspected child maltreatment, in all different professional areas, to consider their legal and ethical obligations to report those suspicions to child protective services (otherwise known as "CPS").

As a lawyer, I've represented the interests of children, their parents, and their custodians in custody, visitation, child support, abuse, and neglect cases in New York City Family Court. As a social worker, I've worked with children and families involved in various legal proceedings to ensure that they have an advocate outside of the courthouse and to help secure them access to the resources they needed to support healthy relationships to last a lifetime. As an educator and researcher, I have examined the intricacies of the system of reporting suspected child maltreatment and designed curricula that help professional reporters understand the decision-making framework to apply to their role. I have co-authored two books on child welfare and mandated reporting with colleagues. This book that you are reading is the culmination of years of study, training, and talking to mandated reporters, just like you, in all stages of their professional careers.

When I work with professional reporters, I see thoughtful, well-meaning people who want to protect children and help families. I develop training and provide consultation services to make sure that these reporters have all the preparation they need to make the tough call, whether that means reporting a case to CPS, or not.

How to use this book?

This book is designed to educate students and professionals in medical and healthcare practice across the United States about what it means to be a mandated reporter and help them consider their professional role as a medical or health professional. This book will provide definitions, explanations, case examples, discussion questions, and questions of all kinds that relate to different aspects of the professional reporting of suspected child maltreatment. This book has been designed to be used as a supplement to other training on reporting child maltreatment, including classroom-based training provided through professional education programs. However, this book can also be used as a stand-alone resource for professionals in various stages of practice who want some more guidance about what to think about when they are considering a report to CPS.

There are many resources out there designed to assist professionals, like you, who are considering making a report to CPS. This book, and related trainings, provides a unique but important perspective to this process. This book starts with YOU.

Any decision to make a report to CPS, or not, is impacted by the personal perspective of the reporter. We each have "lenses" (or perspectives) on the world based on our own life experiences. When we evaluate a situation where child maltreatment might be occurring, it is natural for us to see that child and family through the "lens" of our own experience as a child or a parent (if we are one), or we consider how we might be in that role. Our experiences as children and/or parents are also shaped by our position in the world around us. Our gender identity, age, racial and ethnic identity, and socioeconomic status, amongst other factors, all influence the way we view the situations in front of us.

In some cases, our personal experience and perspective might make us more attuned to the situations we are evaluating, but, in other cases, our personal experience and perspective might cloud or confuse our judgement. When we are considering a report to CPS, it is important that we do so based on our professional judgement and experience and not on our personal judgement. This book will help you consider the impact of your own lenses and positionality, so that when you make the tough call to make a report to CPS, or not, you can be confident that you have made all the appropriate considerations when coming to that determination.

Making the Tough Call is here to help!

This book is part of a larger project called, Making the Tough Call. A training and education initiative, Making the Tough Call provides training, resources, and consultation services to mandated reporters across the country. There is another book in this series aimed at preparation of general categories of mandated reporters, as well as separate books focused on the experiences of mental/ behavioral health professionals and educational/child care professionals. To stay on top of issues related to supporting families and protecting children, sign up for the Making the Tough Call email list on our website at https://www.makingthetoughcall.info and follow us on social media. You can also find additional resources at https://www.makingthetoughcall.info. If you have any questions, you can contact me at ask@makingthetoughcall.info.

"Mandated Reporters": Professional Reporters of Suspected Child Maltreatment

Let's get started. Many professionals across the United States know that they are "mandated reporters." But what does "mandated reporting" mean?

What is "Mandated Reporting"?

"Mandated reporting" refers to the legal obligation of certain individuals to report suspicions of maltreatment to governmental authorities. Most often, we hear about mandated reporting of suspected child abuse and neglect. Another form of mandated reporting relates to suspicions of physical, emotional, and financial abuse of older adults, otherwise known as "elder abuse." Laws requiring the mandated reporting of elder abuse are less common than laws that require the reporting of suspicions of child maltreatment.

Mandated reporting laws vary from state to state, but, in general, professionals who are likely to come in contact with children and their families are mandated reporters of suspected child maltreatment when they develop those suspicions through their professional role. In all states, the list of mandated reporters includes doctors, nurses, teachers, mental health providers, and social workers, though there are many other professional titles included in many states. The list of mandated reporters in most states is very long. In states like New York and California, there are over 30 different professional titles who are mandated reporters. However, the vast majority of reports come from a handful of sources: schools, medical personnel, and law enforcement.

In some states ALL adults are mandated reporters, regardless of whether they fill a particular professional role. We call these states "universal reporting states." As of 2022, universal reporting states include: Delaware, Florida, Idaho, Indiana, Kentucky, Maryland, Mississippi, Nebraska, New Hampshire, New Jersey, New Mexico, North Carolina, Oklahoma, Rhode Island, Tennessee, Texas, Utah, and Wyoming.

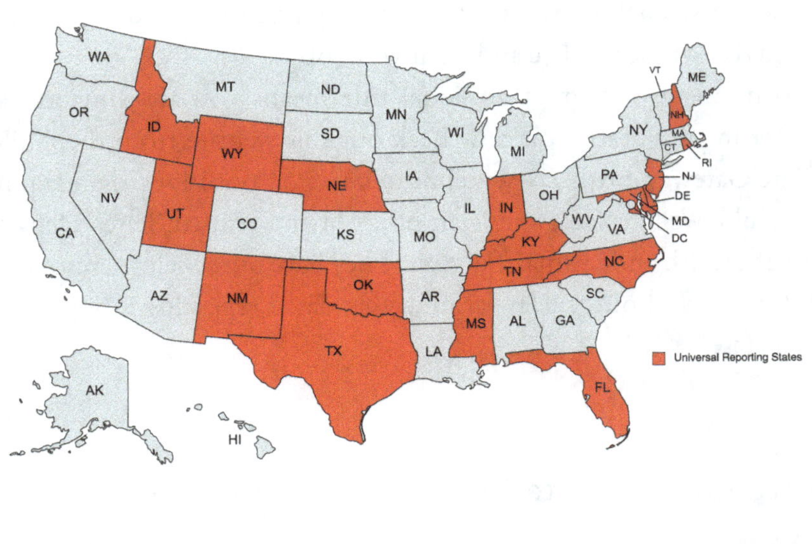

Created with mapchart.net

Universal Reporting States, 2022

If you live or work in a universal reporting state, you are a mandated reporter regardless of your job; you are also a mandated reporter when you're working and when you're not working. For instance, in universal reporting states all adults are required by law to make reports when they have suspicions of child maltreatment about neighbors, family members, even people they see on the street or in the grocery store. In practice, very few people in universal reporting states are aware of this legal obligation, and as a result, the rate of reporting in these states is no different than in non-universal reporting states.

If you live or work in a state without universal reporting requirements, you are not required to make a report to CPS if your suspicions arise from outside your professional role. For instance, in these states no one is required to make reports when they have suspicions of child maltreatment that relate to their neighbors or family members; random citizens in these states are not obligated to make a report about strangers on the street or in the grocery store. However, regardless of what state you live in, you can always choose to make a report to CPS if you have concerns or suspicions; whether you are required to make those reports depends on where you live and what your job is.

To find out if your professional title means you are a mandated reporter in your state, you can check out this website from the Child Welfare Gateway. https://www.childwelfare.gov/pubPDFs/manda.pdf The Child Welfare Gateway is an office of the United States Department of Health and Human Services. They have other helpful resources to inform you about the law around mandated reporting in your particular state.

Where did Mandated Reporting come from?

You may be wondering, where did the idea of mandated reporting come from anyway? Prior to the 1870s, government intervention into family life was very rare, especially in the United States. Parents largely had control over the care of their children, for better and for worse. Starting with the abuse case of Mary Ellen Wilson in New York City in 1875, systems were developed to prevent and respond to child abuse, so that children could be protected. From the 1880s until the 1960s a system of private organizations received reports of suspected child abuse, investigated such reports, and were authorized to remove children into orphanages or foster care to protect them from physical abuse at the hands of their parents. The cases usually involved poor children, often whose parents were believed to abuse alcohol.

In the early 1960s, medical doctors realized that poor children weren't the only victims of child abuse. Easier access to technology allowed doctors to study past injuries. This technology was the X-ray. X-ray examinations allowed doctors to see that many children from middle and upper socio-economic households had repeated fractures of various bones which could only be explained by physical abuse. A doctor named C. Henry Kempe and his colleagues coined a term in a 1962 article in the *Journal of the American Medical Association* to describe a child who had suffered this kind of repeated abuse. Kempe et al. declared that such a child was said to be a victim of "battered child syndrome."

Growing concern for battered children in the 1960s resulted in the development of government intervention to protect children from abuse. This was when the idea of "mandated reporting" was born. Doctors, united under the leadership of the American Medical Association, used their policy advocacy skills and lobbied state and federal governments to require them to make reports of suspected abuse. The first mandated reporting laws were based on the belief that if society could require professionals who have substantial contact with children and families to report suspected child abuse, the government could step in and protect children before they are irreversibly harmed.

By 1967, all 50 states and the District of Columbia passed legislation requiring doctors and other medical personnel to report suspected child maltreatment. Within five years after passing mandatory reporting legislation in New York State, child fatalities dropped by 50%. Mandated reporting laws seemed to be working, and so these laws were quickly expanded across the country.

In the early 1970s, responding to growing nationwide concern for "battered children," the federal government passed the first universal child welfare law, the Child Abuse Prevention and Treatment Act of 1974, or CAPTA. CAPTA is an expansive law that is still in effect today with many modifications taking effect over time. Amongst many other provisions, CAPTA provided for a relative level of uniformity in mandated reporting laws across the country, while simultaneously creating the child protective services system (CPS) that still exists today.

The original mandated reporting laws, and the related focus of CAPTA in the early 1970s, were limited in scope. For instance, original mandated reporting laws only required doctors and medical personnel to report their suspicions to CPS. The list of who is a mandated reporter and what is reportable has grown since 1974. Additionally, these first laws focused on protecting children from physical abuse, not other forms of maltreatment like neglect or emotional abuse. Very quickly, mandated reporting laws expanded, but not necessarily uniformly across the country. Who is a mandated reporter and what types of maltreatment are required to be reported is much more broadly defined than original expectations in the 1970s.

What are Mandated Reporters required to do?

Level of Suspicion

Mandated reporters are required by the law in their state to log suspicions of child maltreatment with the appropriate governmental authorities (usually CPS) when their concerns meet a state-specific threshold. Their concerns must also relate to the definitions of child maltreatment identified by law in the specific state. We will discuss general definitions of various types of child maltreatment in Chapter 3.

The most frequent legal threshold for suspicion that requires a mandated reporter to call CPS is "reasonable suspicion." We will explore what "reasonable suspicion" means in Chapter 4. To find out what the specific threshold for suspicion that requires a report in your state, checkout the Mandated Reporter resource from the Child Welfare Gateway.

Not Just Maltreatment; CHILD Maltreatment

It is important to note that throughout this book we are talking about "CHILD" maltreatment. The term "child" is age limited; this means that most states only require reports when an alleged victim is under 18 years old. In some states, certain mandated reporters are required to report elder abuse, or when suspicions relate to maltreatment of incapacitated or vulnerable adults, usually involving people 18 years of age or older with cognitive and/or physical impairments. Elder abuse is not the focus of the present book. We are exclusively focusing on reports of child maltreatment and the systems that respond to those concerns.

Focusing on Family

Mandated reporting laws are generally limited to suspicions of maltreatment occurring in the home environment and perpetrated by parents or other people legally responsible for children in the home. In most states, suspicions of maltreatment by a teacher, coach, or other person are not required of individual mandated reporters. In many states, reports of such concerns are required to be made to police or law enforcement, but at the institutional level, not the individual reporter level. If you have questions about whether you are required to report suspicions of maltreatment occurring outside a home environment by someone other than a parent or other person legally responsible for a child, you can call the state CPS hotline for assistance. You can find the phone number for the CPS hotline in your particular state by conducting an internet search for: "reporting child abuse in [your state]".

What happens if mandated reporters don't make a report when they are legally required to do so?

When a mandated reporter has concerns that meet the legal threshold to require a report to CPS in their state, they can be held legally liable if they do not make that report. Mandated reporters can be held criminally liable for failing to make a report and can be successfully sued for such failure as well. However, it is very rare for a failure to report case to be identified, and even more rare that a mandated reporter is punished for their failure to report.

In order for a mandated reporter to be held liable for failing to make a report, someone else needs to identify the child maltreatment, determine that the particular mandated reporter had the requisite suspicion to require a report to CPS, AND prove that the mandated reporter didn't make that report. This is a pretty complicated set of circumstances, and, thus, there are very few cases where a mandated reporter is found to have failed to make a report.

In the past decade, however, there have been a growing number of related cases of failure to report child sexual abuse in educational, religious, and extra-curricular settings. In these cases, the institutions involved have been held liable for failing to protect children from sexual abuse, but individual mandated reporters were rarely the focus of criminal prosecution or civil liability.

There was a "failure to report" case in New York State in 2006 that focused on both the failure of an institution and individual mandated reporters to contact CPS when they had suspicions. In this case, a 9-year-old girl told her school friends that she had sex with her mother's boyfriend. The friends told their parents, and the parents told school officials. Teachers and other school officials, including the principal, asked the alleged victim about what she reportedly told her friends; the alleged victim denied saying those things and assured school officials that she was safe at home. The school did not make a report to CPS. The mother of the child victim eventually called the police directly with allegations of child sexual abuse against her boyfriend. The criminal investigation into the case against the boyfriend determined that the school knew about the abuse earlier than the mother's call to the police. Criminal charges were filed against the principal for "failure to report." The charges were later dismissed after the principal agreed to share her story in a number of trainings to mandated reporters across New York State. Civil charges were filed by the child victim's mother against the principal and involved teachers. In response to this case, New York State increased training regarding mandated school reporting of child sexual abuse, including updating annual trainings.

Beyond the legal repercussions of a failure to report, there are potential societal repercussions when child maltreatment is ignored; the government cannot act to protect a child until officials know the child is at risk. Under this assumption, when mandated reporters fail to report, the reporter may be allowing abuse or neglect to continue or denying the family access to much needed services and support.

What happens if a mandated reporter makes a report, but maltreatment isn't found to be occurring?

Mandated reporters are often concerned that they can be sued or arrested if they make a report that does not find evidence of maltreatment after investigation. The law in all 50 states protects reporters from liability if their report is unsubstantiated after investigation. The legal concept of "immunity" protects reporters from being sued or arrested, as long as the reporter made a report to CPS because of a legitimate concern for a child.

CAPTA requires states to have laws that protect anyone who makes a good faith report to child protective services through immunity from criminal and civil liability if an investigation by CPS does not find further evidence of child maltreatment. Immunity protects reporters who are mandated to make reports to CPS as well as reporters who are not required by law to make a report, but still do. We will discuss more about investigations and possible outcomes of those investigations in Chapter 7.

Let's consider a vignette about immunity:

I made a report because I suspected that one of my minor patients was being sexually abused. The investigation ended and the report was not substantiated. The parents are furious and told my supervisor that they are going to sue me and the agency. Can they sue? Will I lose in court?

To be clear, in the United States, almost anyone can sue anyone for anything. BUT, most lawyers would not be interested in representing a family looking for retribution against a mandated reporter for making a report to CPS. Immunity laws protect the reporter from liability, so this family will lose in court unless they show that the reporter made the report in "bad faith."

What if someone makes a false report to CPS?

Immunity does not protect EVERYONE. If a reporter makes a report in bad faith, meaning that they made a false report to CPS, they CAN be arrested or successfully sued by the family. A false report involves knowingly providing CPS with information that is not true.

False reporting is most likely to happen in the context of personal relationships between the reporter and the family. The system, unfortunately, sees many cases each year where frustrated neighbors, or angry family members, make a call to CPS in an attempt to harass or disturb a family when there is no actual concern about child maltreatment. These calls result in unnecessary CPS investigations that can be destabilizing and traumatic to parents and children.

Many false reports are made anonymously. Not all states allow reports to be made anonymously. Anonymity in reports to CPS was originally promoted to encourage people to make reports of concern without fear of retribution. However, data on the high rate of anonymous reports show these reports are most likely to lack validity; anonymous reports might be more troubling than helpful. As a result, a number of states are exploring the elimination of anonymous reporting.

Please note, mandated reporters cannot, generally, make anonymous reports. In order to ensure that mandated reporters meet their legal obligation to report suspicions, it is necessary for mandated reporters to provide their name and contact information when making a report to CPS.

One of my colleagues made a physical abuse report about a parent they've been working with. The colleague told me they didn't have any reason to believe there was abuse happening but wanted to scare the parent into shaping up and being a better parent. Can the colleague be arrested? Sued?

This is false reporting. If CPS determines that the colleague made a false report, they could be arrested and successfully sued. Being subjected to a CPS investigation is a stressful situation for parents and children. An investigation can be disruptive to a family unit whether or not maltreatment is occurring. Investigations of false reports can be destabilizing to a family, and, ultimately, children and families are hurt. These results are the opposite of the intention of the purpose of making a report to CPS. Reports should be made only when there is genuine concern for a child's safety or condition. False reports don't just hurt the family in question; they tax an overwhelmed and under-resourced system.

Now that you have some of the important basics about the role of mandated reporters, we will get more in depth about expectations. In the next chapter, we will explore how the professional role of medical and health professionals relates to their obligations as mandated reporters.

Test Questions

1. True/False: Mandated reporting laws are the same across all 50 states.
2. True/False: Mandated reporters must report ALL suspicions of child maltreatment.
3. True/False: If an investigation does not find evidence to support a mandated reporter's concerns, the mandated reporter is protected from legal liability by immunity.
4. True/False: Mandated reporters can be held criminally liable for failing to make a report when the law requires them to.
5. True/False: People who make false reports to child protective services can be held criminally or civilly liable.

Discussion Questions

- When did you first learn that YOU were a mandated reporter? What feelings did you have about your obligations in this role? How have your feelings changed over time?
- Were you surprised that mandated reporting laws have only been around since the 1960s and 1970s? Why? Why not? What else was happening during that time period that might have influenced the emergence of these laws?
- Find out if you live/work in a universal reporting state. Now, consider your obligations in your current state. How would they change if you moved to a state with a different reporting requirement?

Resources

Child Welfare Information Gateway, United States Department of Health & Human Services, Administration on Children and Families, https://www.childwelfare.gov/

Kempe, C.H., Silverman, F.N., Steele, B.F., Droegemueller, W., & Silver, H.K. (1962). The Battered-Child Syndrome. *Journal of the American Medical Association*, 181(1), 17.

2

Focus on Medical and Healthcare Professionals

This book is specifically designed for medical and healthcare professionals, including, but not limited to: nurses, physicians, physician assistants, dentists, dental hygienists, emergency medical technicians, pharmacists, dietitians, physical therapists, occupational therapists, and medical technologists. This book is also appropriate to any other person employed in fields related to these professions who is identified as a mandated reporter by the law in their state. This book is designed to be helpful for those studying to be medical and healthcare professionals, as well as those already practicing in the field.

Medical and healthcare professionals are unique in your role as mandated reporters. For many of you, your professional education teaches you how to assess and evaluate your patients. Your skills at deduction and your training in working with patients are invaluable tools that can be used to protect children and support families, but being a mandated reporter is not your only professional obligation. Medical and healthcare professionals need to balance their professional obligations to provide the care they are employed to provide, with their legal and ethical obligations to report appropriate suspicions of child maltreatment to child protective services.

Reporting of Child Maltreatment by Medical and Healthcare Professionals

Medical and healthcare professionals are responsible for making approximately 11% of reports to CPS on an annual basis; schools make about 21% of reports; law enforcement makes about 19% of reports; and, mental/behavioral health professionals make about 6% of reports. Since there are approximately 4 million reports to CPS each year, it means that medical and healthcare professionals make at least 440,000 of those reports.

Research on the quality of reports from medical and healthcare professionals, however, is concerning. The likelihood of reports from medical and healthcare professionals being substantiated after investigation is pretty low. While research finds that reports from medical and healthcare professionals are amongst those most likely coming from professional report sources to be substantiated after investigation, nearly three-quarters of reports from medical and healthcare professionals are NOT supported by evidence gathered through an investigation. That means that more than 300,000 reports from medical and healthcare professionals are unsubstantiated each year!

Reports of neglect that are made by medical and healthcare professionals are the LEAST likely category of maltreatment reported to be substantiated after investigation. As we will discuss in Chapter 4, neglect is the form of maltreatment most difficult to identify, for a variety of reasons. Due to the low substantiation rates of neglect reports from medical and healthcare professionals, it is even more important for this group to be thoughtful about their role as mandated reporters and be as well prepared as possible to meet their legal and ethical obligations to their patients.

Ethics of Medical and Healthcare Professionals

Central to the role of any medical or healthcare professional is your orientation to your ethical responsibilities. Professionals learn about ethical responsibilities in professional training programs, but continue to be held to those standards in practice.

Each professional group has at least one central "Code of Ethics". *The Code of Ethics for Nurses* is authored and maintained by the American Nurses Association (ANA). The American Medical Association (AMA) authors and maintains the *Medical Code of Ethics*. The American Academy of Physician Assistants authors and maintains the *Guidelines for Ethical Conduct for the PA Profession*. The list goes on... Additionally, sub groups within each profession may have codes of ethics and conduct that further delineate specialized responsibilities based on the populations of patients that they work with, the systems that they work within, or the nature of the communities that they serve.

All these ethical codes outline the guiding principles of professions and the priorities for navigating ethical conflicts. These codes of ethics often directly refer to the conundrum faced when the law requires the professional to make reports of suspected child maltreatment to child protective services. However, the decision to report is ultimately left to the individual professional to discern. This book will help you consider your ethical obligations, along with the facts presented to you, and provide you with a framework to guide your decision making.

Law and Professional Ethics Related to Mandated Reporting

A major ethical responsibility all medical and healthcare professionals learn about early and often in our professional training is "patient confidentiality." You're told: "Don't talk about your patients with friends or family"; "Don't discuss patients in the hallway or the elevator"; and so on. And yet, as mandated reporters, we're required by law to report suspicions of child abuse and neglect. Isn't there are an ethical conflict created when the law requires us to breach patient confidentiality? The short answer is: "Yes." The longer answer is: "It's complicated." Let's explore the complication.

Responsibility to Keep Patient Information Confidential

The obligation of medical and healthcare professionals related to "patient confidentiality" means that much of the information shared within the patient-professional relationship should not be shared outside that relationship. The expectation is that when a patient shares information with a healthcare professional, the professional will not reveal this information to others. The purpose of patient confidentiality is to encourage patients to share information that may be embarrassing, or even self-incriminating, but necessary to inform appropriate medical intervention. Through the sharing of such information, the healthcare professional can help the patient address a condition, concern, or problem the patient may be experiencing.

The professional's obligation to keep patient information confidential is not only supported through state and federal law, but it is also discussed extensively in professional codes of ethics. However, both the law and all ethical codes provide exceptions to patient confidentiality for reporting suspicions of child maltreatment.

HIPAA

HIPAA stands for the Health Insurance Portability and Accountability Act of 1996. HIPAA is a federal law passed to promote greater sensitivity and awareness of the protection of private patient/patient information collected during physical, behavioral, and mental healthcare. Contrary to popular understanding, HIPAA didn't set the high level of protection healthcare records deserve. Instead, HIPAA outlined a process through which patients have to be informed about their rights and acknowledge them. The HIPAA forms required at most medical and healthcare professional visits generally explain how patient information will be shared within a healthcare setting or with insurance companies.

Medical and healthcare professionals often ask: "Doesn't HIPAA say I can't share patient records without a written release? So, how am I allowed to make a report to CPS?" Mandated reporting laws existed before HIPAA was passed in1996. So, the framers of HIPAA specifically provided an exception to the requirement for release of confidential information that acknowledges the obligation of mandated reporters to breach patient confidentiality in order to make reports to CPS. In fact, if you read the details on many HIPAA forms, or the text of the HIPAA legislation itself, you'll see that HIPAA specifically provides for disclosure of patient/patient information without consent when the professional is legally required to report to public health and other government authorities. So, mandated reporting obligations do not conflict with HIPAA.

Substance Abuse Treatment Records

Federal law (42 CFR 2) protects substance abuse treatment records at a different level than other medical records. The law, originally passed in 1975, acknowledged that people would be more likely to seek treatment for substance use disorders if the records of such treatment were held to a higher standard of confidentiality. However, the law provides the same type of exception to patient confidentiality as HIPAA does. There is a stated exception to confidentiality in the law that allows for sharing information when the provider is otherwise required to make a disclosure to satisfy a legitimate government purpose, like making a report to CPS.

Some professionals might think: "Well, of course substance abuse treatment providers have to make reports to CPS because drug use by parents is bad." While substance use disorders are not ideal, especially when someone has a parental responsibility, a substance use disorder, alone, is not child maltreatment.

To be clear, when a substance abuse treatment provider is a mandated reporter in a particular state, and they develop the requisite legal level of suspicion to require a report to CPS, the federal law protecting substance abuse treatment records does not preclude the provider from making such a report.

Professional Ethics

Ethical guidelines that relate to medical and healthcare practice have a lot to say about defining and, thereby, protecting patient confidentiality. The ANA Code of Ethics for Nurses, Provision 3.1, recognizes that nurses have a duty to maintain confidentiality of patient information. "The nurse has a duty to maintain confidentiality of all patient information, both personal and clinical in the work setting and off duty in all venues including social media or any other means of communication" (ANA, 2015). The AMA Code of Medical Ethics, Opinion 3.2.1, provides: "[p]hysicians... have an ethical obligation to preserve the confidentiality of information gathered in association with the care of the patient. In general, patients are entitled to decide whether and to whom their personal health information is disclosed" (AMA, 2001). The Code of Ethics for the Physical Therapist, maintained by the American Physical Therapy Association (APTA) provides: "[p]hysical therapists shall protect confidential patient and client information and may disclose confidential information to appropriate authorities only when allowed or as required by law" (APTA, n.d.).

The law and ethical codes both provide exceptions to professional obligations to preserve patient confidentiality when faced with the legal requirement to report suspicions of child maltreatment to CPS. For instance, the ANA Code of Ethics provide: "[t]he duty to maintain confidentiality is not absolute and may be limited, as necessary, to protect the patient or other parties, or by law or regulation such as mandated reporting for safety or public health reasons" (ANA, 2015). The AMA Code of Medical Ethics, Opinion 3.2.1 (d) allows physicians to "disclose personal health information without the specific consent of the patient [t]o appropriate authorities when disclosure is required by law" (AMA, 2001). However, professionals have additional obligations that relate to helping patients understand the limits of confidentiality, as well as for minimizing disclosures when breaching confidentiality is otherwise required. We will discuss these considerations in Chapter 7.

Confidentiality vs. Privilege

Another questions I often hear is: "Is there a difference between confidentiality and privilege? I know they both relate to the privacy of what our patients tell us, but do the terms mean the same thing?" Confidentiality and privilege are not the same concept, but they are related.

Confidentiality relates to the responsibility of professionals to keep patient information private, as provided through our ethical code and the law. Privilege relates to the obligation of professionals to protect this information from being introduced during a legal proceeding. The protection provided by privilege derives from a confidential relationship, but the protection of privilege can only be asserted in relation to a legal proceeding.

Confidentiality is a broad term, with many exceptions. Privilege, in the context of court proceedings, is very limited. There are a limited number of privileges recognized in most courts. Nurses, physicians, physician assistants, dentists and chiropractors all have privileged relationships with their patients. There is a lawyer-patient privilege. There's a priest-penitent privilege, which also extends to other religious leaders and their relationship with congregants seeking counsel. There is also a marital privilege. Then, there is a therapist-patient privilege.

Most importantly, the concept of privilege does not preclude a mandated reporter in any confidential relationship from legally and ethically making a report to CPS. Privilege can, however, impact the extent to which a medical or healthcare professional participates as a witness in any resulting court case on child maltreatment.

The Importance of Informed Consent

Balancing the ethical responsibility to protect patient confidentiality and the legal obligation to protect children from harm can be very difficult, even for professionals with decades of experience. How can you navigate these obligations in the best way possible? First things first, you start at the beginning of the relationship with your patient by incorporating a discussion of the limits to confidentiality with your patient through "informed consent".

Informed consent is the process through which professionals discuss with patients the nature of the professional-patient relationship. Through informed consent, the professional and patient outline what the patient should expect from the professional relationship, as well as what the professional expects from the patient's participation.

Informed consent often includes a discussion of basic protocols, like how to make or cancel appointments, or the best way to contact the professional with a question or concern. The process should also involve outlining what work will be done with and for the patient and what expectations there are for patient involvement. Integral to the informed consent process is a discussion of patient confidentiality.

Using simple language, appropriate to the developmental and language needs of the patient, the professional needs to explain to the patient that they will generally keep information private, but that there are specific instances when the professional is required to break patient confidentiality. For instance, it is important to inform the patient that you are legally obligated to breach patient confidentiality to protect identifiable people from harm, including the patient. It is at this point that you should highlight that if you suspect child maltreatment based on information received from the patient, you must breach patient confidentiality to make a report to suspected child protective services.

It is important to clarify with the patient that the professional may have to report suspected child abuse or neglect based on what the patient says even if the patient is neither the victim nor the perpetrator.

In other words, the professional may (depending on the state they reside in) have to make a report involving people they have never met.

In some agencies or practice settings informed consent involves the patient signing a form that acknowledges receipt of certain information. See the provided example of informed consent language, below. While a written tool is a good idea, it is important that there be additional methods for ensuring informed consent.

Example of Informed Consent Language

[We] value the relationships we have with our patients, and hold information shared with us through our work as confidential. [We] will not share information outside the professional relationship, except for specific circumstances. Those circumstances include when the patient requests of us that [we] share such information, through a release of information process. Also, under state law, [we] must report information about known or reasonably suspected harm to a child including physical, sexual, and/or emotional abuse, as well as neglect. [We may be] also required to disclose patient confidential information when we have reason to believe that a patient may harm themselves or somebody else. When [we] determine that [we] must disclose patient confidential information due to a legal obligation, [we] make every effort to ensure that [we] only share information necessary to effectuate our responsibilities under the law, and strive to retain as much confidential information about our patient as possible. If you have any questions about the circumstances under which we must disclose confidential information, please talk to [us].

(Adjust "we" and "us" as appropriate to your setting and organization.)

In all cases, with or without written informed consent tools, the professional and patient should discuss expectations for confidentiality and when confidentiality will be breached. The professional should use language that the patient can understand. So, the professional can say that they will keep information "private" or "between the two of us." But it is very important that the professional makes it clear that there may be times when the "private" information will be shared with others. Basic language can be used, such as: "I will have to share this private information if I think that you are going to hurt yourself or hurt someone else or if I think someone may be hurting you or someone else."

As with other forms of communication with patients, it is important to ensure that the patient understands what you outline through informed consent. For work with patients for whom English is not their primary language, it is important to provide the opportunity for this process in a language more appropriate to their ability to understand at a deeper level.

With child patients, or patients with impaired cognitive ability, you can start by asking them if they understand, but it is best to follow up. You can ask a question like: "If a child told me that someone was hurting him at home, would I keep that private?" And then you can explain who you would report to and why, highlighting that child protective services could then help protect that patient from being hurt again.

It is possible that by explaining to your patient the limits of confidentiality, they may choose not to disclose information that would warrant you to make a report to child protective services. It is important to remember that it is the patient's right to choose what information to share with you; that is part of the patient's right to "self-determination" or a reflection of their "autonomy." Both self-determination and autonomy of the patient are important ethical principles highlighted in the codes of most medical and healthcare professions.

Informed consent is most often thought of in the context of the "intake" stage with a patient at the beginning of the professional relationship. However, in order to be effective, informed consent should be seen as an ONGOING process. Informed consent can be integrated at regular/periodic intervals throughout a professional relationship.

Professional Autonomy

In this chapter we've explored the obligations of professionals to their patients. We've specifically discussed the right of patients to autonomy and self-determination and the impact those rights might have on our ability to perform our role as mandated reporters. It is also important to explore the impact of our role as mandated reporters on our own autonomy, our professional autonomy.

Medical and healthcare professionals are often autonomous in your work. You use your skills at assessment, intervention, and evaluation to determine, in conjunction with your patients, colleagues, and supervisors, what is the appropriate course of practice with a particular patient. There is a high level of responsibility you have provide the appropriate level of skill to make these decisions. In order to assert this responsibility, you must earn certain degrees, and pass certain exams, and participate in continuing education programming throughout your careers.

There are a few situations where your legal and ethical obligations infringe on your ability to be autonomous professionals. A major limitation to your professional practice, likely, comes from funding sources; the level of insurance coverage a patient has might limit the choices for what interventions they can afford. As a result, the medical or healthcare professional may not have the full scope of autonomy that we ideally would want to address the patient's condition.

Another situation where our legal and ethical obligations infringe on our ability to be autonomous professionals is when we are required by law to make reports to CPS. Don't get me wrong. I am NOT saying that medical and healthcare professionals shouldn't make reports to CPS, especially when they believe that such a report will protect a child and help a family. What I AM saying is that when anyone is required to do something, it means that they lose their ability to make reasoned decisions which professionals, in particular, are trained for and capable of making.

As you continue to read this book, I encourage you to think about situations when you feel the decision to report to CPS is congruent with the requirement to make a report to CPS and when the decision and the requirement might be in conflict with your notion of best practices. After all, medical and healthcare professionals are tasked with some serious responsibilities. The more thoughtful you are about your work, the more likely you are to do that for which you came to this career in the first place: to help people.

Test Questions

Which of the following plans for providing informed consent is most appropriate for working with children?

a. Have them sign a form that lists all the situations in which you would have to tell other people what they tell you
b. Tell the child that you will never tell anyone what they tell you.
c. Explain to the child that you will try to keep information they share with you private, but there are some times when you will have to tell other people what they tell you.
d. Don't discuss informed consent with children under 5 years old.
e. Don't discuss informed consent with children under 10 years old.

Which of the following plans for providing informed consent is most appropriate for working with adults with cognitive impairment?

a. Have them sign a form that lists all the situations in which you would have to tell other people what they tell you.
b. Tell the patient that you will never tell anyone what they tell you.
c. Explain to the patient that you will try to keep information they share with you private, but there are some times when you will have to tell other people what they tell you.
d. Don't discuss informed consent with adult patients with cognitive impairment.
e. Get informed consent from the patient's legal guardian.

Which of the following best describes the difference between confidentiality and privilege?

    a. Privilege derives from a relationship that includes an expectation that information passed within the relationship will remain confidential.
    b. Confidentiality is more important than privilege.
    c. Privilege is more important than confidentiality.
    d. In order to have confidentiality, there must be a privilege.
    e. Confidentiality only matters in a court case.

Which of the following relationships is NOT recognized as privileged in court?

    a. Teacher-Student
    b. Doctor-Patient
    c. Lawyer-patient
    d. Therapist-patient
    e. Priest-Penitent

Which of the following provides an exception to patient confidentiality in order to make reports to CPS?

    a. Laws protecting substance abuse treatment records
    b. HIPAA
    c. ANA Code of Ethics for Nurses
    d. AMA Principles of Medical Ethics
    e. All of these rules provide an exception to patient confidentiality in order to make reports to CPS.

Discussion Questions

- Role-play your informed discussion conversation with a new patient who is a parent to young children. How would this conversation differ if you were providing informed consent to a toddler? A second grader? An adolescent? An older adult? A cognitively impaired patient?
- How might your decision to breach patient confidentiality to make a report impact your relationship with your patient?

References & Resources

American Medical Association (2001). Principles of medical ethics. https://www.ama-assn.org/sites/ama-assn.org/files/corp/media-browser/principles-of-medical-ethics.pdf

American Nurses Association. (2015). Code of ethics for nurses with interpretive statements. https://www.nursingworld.org/practice-policy/nursing-excellence/ethics/code-of-ethics-for-nurses/coe-view-only/

American Physical Therapy Association. (n.d.). Code of ethics for the physical therapist. Retrieved from: http://www.apta.org/uploaded-Files/APTAorg/About_Us/Policies/Ethics/CodeofEthics.pdf

Confidentiality of Substance Use Disorder Patient Records (2017). 42 CFR 2.

U.S. Department of Health and Human Services, Administration on Children, Youth andFamilies (2020). Child Maltreatment 2019 (Washington, DC: U.S. Government Printing Office) https://www.acf.hhs.gov/sites/default/files/documents/cb/cm2019.pdf

3 █

Challenges of Reporting Child Maltreatment

Protecting children from harm is the ultimate goal of the child welfare system and the reason for mandated reporting. Mandated reporting legislation was swiftly passed into law in all 50 states in the 1960s because everyone can agree that children should be protected from harm, whenever possible. Unfortunately, there are often unforeseen consequences when trying to meet any goal, even when there are the best of intentions.

There are many challenges to child maltreatment reporting. Some are personal or professional for the reporter, and others are structural and systemic. Mandated reporting is challenging, and the child protection system that is connected to the role has its own challenges. This chapter will explore some challenges that exist at various levels related to the reporting of suspected child maltreatment. The more you think about them, the more challenges you might identify, but, hopefully, the more likely you will start to find some solutions as well.

Role Challenges of Mandated Reporters

Mandated reporting is not easy. Most mandated reporters are confused about their role. Some mandated reporters don't know that they're mandated reporters. Some mandated reporters don't understand their legal obligations. Some mandated reporters don't know what they're supposed to be looking for. They don't know what they're supposed to do if they have suspicions. They're concerned about making a bad report. They're concerned that they'll get in trouble if they make a report and they're wrong. They're concerned that making a report won't actually help the child or family as they are hoping a report will. The challenges in understanding the role of mandated reporter result in problems, including two specific phenomena: "under-reporting" and "over-reporting."

"Under-reporting"

Research shows that many mandated reporters do not report cases where they suspect child maltreatment. There are many reasons mandated reporters cite for not reporting:

- They don't know what's reportable;
- They don't know the difference between corporal punishment and physical abuse;
- The concept of neglect is especially confusing;
- They don't know how to make a report;
- They believe they need more evidence of maltreatment before calling CPS;
- They are concerned about the impact of a report on their relationship with the child and family; and lastly,
- Some argue that reporting may produce more harm than good.

No matter what the reason for not reporting suspected maltreatment, it is very possible that many children are left at risk of harm because many professional reporters do not report their suspicions even though they are legally obligated to do so. More training and resources are needed to help inform and guide reporters about how to identify and respond to child maltreatment.

"Over-reporting"

Under-reporting is not the only problem with the current state of reporting to CPS. Over-reporting of suspicions is also a problem. Fewer than 20% of reports to CPS result in a determination after investigation that a child is a victim of maltreatment. This means that 80% of families that get reported are not determined to have experienced maltreatment. With over 4 million reports to CPS a year, that means over 3 million families who might not need any intervention at all face a CPS report and resulting investigation.

It is important to clarify that there are many reasons why an investigation might be closed without determining that maltreatment has occurred.

No Maltreatment Occurring

No maltreatment occurring is an obvious reason to close a report without determining child maltreatment occurred. If there is no maltreatment occurring, we hope that the investigation will be closed without a finding to the contrary.

Genuine Concern

Many reports to CPS that are ultimately determined to not include maltreatment are made by concerned professional and non-professional reporters who genuinely believe a family needs help. These reporters, however, might not be aware of the definitions of child maltreatment, or they might be confusing concern for a child or family with suspicion of child maltreatment. As a result, these reporters make reports of a situation that does not rise to the level of child maltreatment.

False Reports

Another source of reports where no maltreatment is occurring are "false reports." As discussed in Chapter 1, false reports are usually made by non-professional sources seeking to disrupt or harass families for personal reasons. While false reports make up a small minority of cases that get investigated, they are very problematic. False reports are often made by anonymous reporters, making them hard to prosecute, punish, and prevent. False reports that are made by reporters who share their name and contact information with CPS are rarely prosecuted for their infractions, either, because it is hard to prove that the reporter knowingly and willingly lied.

Resulting Disruptions to Families and System

In cases where no maltreatment is occurring, but a report is nonetheless made, children and families suffer from unwarranted intrusion and disruption as a result of CPS investigations. All CPS investigations involve interviewing family members, and they often involve communicating with collateral contacts, like school personnel and neighbors. Parents who are investigated by CPS often feel like they have to defend themselves and prove that they care about their children; this is a normal response. When maltreatment is occurring, the stress and trauma that the investigatory process can cause is, arguably, justified because the goal is ultimately protecting children. But, when maltreatment is NOT occurring, the stress and trauma that the investigatory process can cause to a family is, arguably, NOT justified.

In addition to the intrusion and stress caused by these reports, reports made when no maltreatment is occurring add pressure to an already overburdened child protection system. Each report that is taken by CPS is required to be investigated. Unnecessary reports overwhelm systems and services that are designed to protect at-risk children and families, making it less likely that families that need help get help.

How to Reduce Over-Reporting

To reduce the likelihood of these kinds of reports, training and other forms of access to information (like this book) that encourage reporters to be thoughtful and contemplative in the process of reporting are needed. Professional and non-professional reporters would also benefit from information on resources they can offer to help families receive the support they might need to function at their highest potential. In other words, if reporters had another option than calling CPS every time they had a concern, reserving reports for when concerns rise to a higher level of suspicion, there might be fewer reports to CPS made where no maltreatment was occurring, and more families might receive the assistance they need, as a result.

Maltreatment Occurring, BUT Investigation Doesn't Find Enough Evidence

There are times when an investigation of a report to CPS does not conclude maltreatment is occurring, but, in fact, there is maltreatment occurring. Generally, these are situations where an investigation does not yield enough evidence of maltreatment. There are a few reasons why an investigation might not find adequate evidence of maltreatment even though it is occurring.

"Burden of Proof"

In order for an investigation of a CPS report to conclude with a determination that child maltreatment has occurred, evidence must be collected during the investigation that meets a certain legal threshold, referred to as a "burden of proof." The evidentiary threshold for the burden of proof needed to determine after a CPS investigation that child maltreatment has occurred varies by state. Some states use a very low threshold, like "reasonable evidence" or "some credible evidence." Other states use higher standards commonly found in civil court proceedings, like "preponderance of the evidence" and "clear and convincing evidence." No state uses the threshold reserved for criminal court cases, as in "beyond a reasonable doubt." It is important to note that states with higher evidentiary thresholds for determining child maltreatment has occurred have lower proportions of reports deemed to involve child maltreatment. Since state standards differ, it is possible that an investigation in one state would yield a determination of child maltreatment, but an investigation finding the same evidence in a neighboring state would NOT yield the same determination.

Quality of CPS Investigation

Regardless of the threshold for determining the outcome of an investigation, the quality of investigations by CPS, as well as the depth of CPS's access to information, impact the likelihood that an investigation will result in a determination that child maltreatment exists. Investigation quality and access to information can be impacted by a number of factors.

The quality of an investigation may be impacted by the preparation of workers responsible for the process. For instance, you might not realize that the standards for education and training in order to become a CPS worker differ by state and jurisdiction. You might assume that in order to be a CPS worker you need to have a degree in social work, psychology, or human behavior; however, such degrees are not the standard for CPS workers.

Most generally, CPS workers are expected to have some level of college education, preferably completion of a bachelor's degree. Many jurisdictions have hiring preferences for CPS workers with a background, or a minimum number of college credits, in social work, human behavior, psychology, or sociology; there is no uniform minimum qualification for these positions across the country. The lack of uniformly high standards for professional preparation for CPS positions is compounded by the relatively low salary these positions earn, the large caseloads, and the high levels of stress experienced by those who serve in these positions. As a result, there are high rates of burnout and turnover in the CPS workforce. Efforts in some states and local jurisdictions to professionalize the child protection workforce have seen successes.

More research and investment are warranted to continue to address these professionalization concerns.

Lack of Evidence

An investigation might not find sufficient evidence of maltreatment, even when it is occurring, because such evidence doesn't exist, or it is not easily accessed. As we will learn in the next chapter, some forms of maltreatment are hard to identify because of lack of proof. Some forms of maltreatment have physical indicators, like injuries, but most forms of maltreatment do not. Most forms of maltreatment are defined and characterized by conditions that are hard, if not impossible, to prove. We will discuss the challenges related to identifying indicators of maltreatment in the coming sections.

Concerns for Social and Racial Justice

Under- and over-reporting are problems that are additionally compounded by the resulting concerns for social and racial justice. Concern for justice in reporting is not new; policymakers who designed the original mandated reporting legislation in the 1960s and 1970s were concerned that the new system would specifically have negative impact on low-income families, which they knew included a higher proportion of Black/African-American families. The Indian Child Welfare Act (ICWA) of 1978 similarly identified systemic racial injustice experienced by Native American, Indian American and Indigenous identifying families. ICWA attempted to respond to centuries of intergenerational disruption to these communities caused by the federal, state, and local levels of government. In Chapter 4, we will discuss how poverty relates to the definition of child neglect. Here, we are focusing on the relationship of social and racial justice in reporting any form of child maltreatment.

Economic Justice

Families living in poverty, and otherwise economically disenfranchised families, are believed to be more likely to come into contact with mandated reporters, like social service workers, than wealthier families. As a result, families with lower incomes were thought to face a higher probability that they would be reported to CPS. The original concerns, however, were related to access to mandated reporters and not focused on potential for bias impacting reporting.

Over the past 50 years, research has shown that professional reporters may be less likely to report wealthier families, even when they have reasonable suspicion. Professional reporters may feel that the wealthier family does not need to be involved in CPS; instead, the reporters may choose to work with the family to improve their functioning without alerting CPS. Other reporters may choose not to report wealthier families because they are concerned that a report will result in the loss of clients, patients, or customers who no longer trust the service provider to be discreet.

To compound the potential under-reporting of concerns related to wealthier families, professional reporters might also be more willing to report poor families due to implicit bias. Reporters, unknowingly and unwittingly in some cases, may judge families with less economic security more harshly than wealthier families facing the same struggles. Reporters might think that families with lower levels of economic security are less likely to be able to manage the struggles and challenges their families face. As a result, reporters might feel more comfortable making reports to CPS of families that have less economic security.

Racial Justice

Children who identify as Black, Indigenous, and People of Color (BIPOC), specifically Black/African-American, Latino/Latinx/Hispanic and Native American/American-Indian/Alaskan Native children, are reported at a higher rate than they are found in the general population at either the national, state, or local level; this is called "over-representation" and/or "racial disproportionality." Black children, in particular, make up more than 20% of reports to CPS across the country each year, but only represent 15% of the children in the United States. Research in New York State found Black children were seven times more likely to be reported to CPS than White children in the state. And, research suggests that more than half of Black families are investigated by CPS at some point in a child's life. In fact, Black children are not only over-represented in reports to CPS, but at all phases of a child protection case, including substantiation after investigation, removal from caretakers, and termination of parental rights.

These statistics make it seem like BIPOC children are more likely than White children to be abused or neglected, but that's not necessarily true. Remember, more than 2/3 of reports do not find evidence of maltreatment after investigation; that means a lot of families of color are being investigated by CPS, but without resulting need for intervention.

Research suggests that racially disproportionate reporting is due, in part, to disproportionate rates of poverty amongst BIPOC families. However, research over the past 20 years has found that implicit and explicit bias also contribute to racially disproportionate reporting.

Studies have found that Black and Hispanic children who present to the emergency rooms of hospitals with minor head trauma are two to four times more likely to be evaluated and reported for suspected abusive head trauma than White children, regardless of the circumstances of their presenting injury. Additional research shows a similar pattern in reporting Black mothers for drug use when the hospital records a positive toxicology for illicit drugs found in a newborn's blood test shortly after birth. Contrary to popular belief, there is no law that requires hospitals to report these positive tests to CPS, though some hospitals have stated policy to report all such tests. However, in practice, research shows hospitals are less likely to report White mothers than Black mothers. As a result of research findings like these, the American Academy of Pediatrics made the following statement in 2021:

*" Systemic racism and implicit bias play key roles in who "
faces a child protective services investigation and exacer-
bates inequities. It is clear that these factors cause significant harm, both by over-investigating families of color and
by over-burdening the child protective services system in
ways that undermine its ability to appropriately identify
and respond to situations where children face credible risk
of injury and fatality.*

Although intended to protect children and families, mandated reporting of child maltreatment is likely contributing to institutional and
systemic racism in the child protective system. With these statistics and
statements in mind, reporters should pay special attention to making
sure that they are only considering the facts and observations available
to them when deciding whether to make a report to CPS. It is impera-
tive for reporters to ensure they are not making a judgement about a
child, or their family, due to racial or ethnic identity. We will explore
how to include concern for implicit and explicit bias when we outline a
framework for decision making in Chapter 5.

Impact of COVID

This book is being published with the COVID pandemic still raging
on. There is a lot of theory out there about the impact of COVID on
child maltreatment, and ultimately on reports of child maltreatment,
but very little data. Preliminary research based on evidence from hospitals suggests that child physical abuse might have increased during the
period of school shutdowns. We also know that widespread shutdowns
of schools and services resulted in a drastic plummeting of reports to
CPS in 2020. It is important to note, however, that we will not know
for many years the impact that the COVID pandemic has had on
the incidence and prevalence of child maltreatment, and the resulting
impact on children.

Larger CPS Systems Issues

Ultimately, the largest challenges to the CPS system are structural. Even though state governments took on responsibility for child welfare and child protection in the 1960s, and the federal government began subsidizing those systems in the 1970s, there have never been adequate funding levels of CPS, especially in regard to services aimed at preventing child maltreatment and supporting families.

The good news is that rates of child maltreatment have been trending downward, especially related to evidence of physical and sexual abuse. There is also a growing awareness of the problems inherent in the current structure of CPS. As a result, there are more cohesive voices demanding change, at many levels. Chapter 8 will explore ways mandated reporters can advocate for system improvements that will support everyone's ultimate goal of protecting children, and supporting families.

Test Questions

True/False: Confusion about the role of mandated reporters can lead to under-reporting of suspicions to CPS.

Approximately, what proportion of CPS investigations are closed without determining that maltreatment has occurred?

    a. 80%
    b. 50%
    c. 20%
    d. 10%

Which of the following is NOT a reason that CPS investigations are closed without determining that maltreatment has occurred?

    a. False reports
    b. Low quality CPS investigations
    c. Failure of mandated reporters to report suspicions

d. Lack of access to evidence

African-American children are over-represented in which of the following stages of the child protective system?

a. Reporting
b. Substantiation after investigation
c. Removal from caretakers
d. Termination of parental rights
e. All of the above

Which of the following statements about COVID and child maltreatment is true?

a. Reports of child maltreatment plummeted during the COVID lockdowns.
b. More cases of physical abuse were identified in emergency rooms during the COVID lockdowns than before COVID.
c. We won't know the true impact of the COVID pandemic on child maltreatment for many years to come.
d. All of the answers are correct

Discussion Questions

- Were you surprised to hear about the social and racial justice concerns in reporting suspicions of child maltreatment? Why or why not?
- No one in the child protection system considered that a pandemic would upend the system's functioning. Now we know there is great potential for future disruption, even when we can't predict when or what will occur. How should we prepare for foreseeable societal concerns, like climate change, that will likely

impact the ability of the child protection system to respond to families in need?

Important Organizations

Casey Family Programs, https://www.casey.org/.

Kempe Center for the Prevention and Treatment of Child Abuse and Neglect, at the University of Colorado, School of Medicine, https://medschool.cuanschutz.edu/pediatrics/sections/child-abuse-and-neglect-kempe-center

National Coalition for Child Protection Reform, https://nccpr.org/.

Rise Magazine, https://www.risemagazine.org.

References

Besharov, D.J. & Laumann, L.A. (1996). Child abuse reporting. *Society*. May/June 1996.

Chasnoff, I.J., Landress, H.J., & Barrett M.E. (1990). The prevalence of illicit-drug or alcohol use during pregnancy and discrepancies in mandatory reporting in Pinellas County, Florida. *New England Journal of Medicine*, Apr 26;322(17):1202-6. doi: 10.1056/NEJM199004263221706. PMID: 2325711.

Higgins, D. J., & McCabe, M. P. (2000). Multi-type maltreatment and the long-term adjustment of adults. *Child Abuse Review: Journal of the British Association for the Study and Prevention of Child Abuse and Neglect*, 9(1), 6-18.

Hutchison, E. D. (1993). Mandatory reporting laws: Child protective case finding gone awry? *Social Work*, 38(1), 56-63.

Hymel, K.P., Laskey, A.L., Crowell, K.R., Wang, M., Armijo-Garcia, V., Frazier, T.N., Tieves, K.S., Foster, R., Weeks, K.; Pediatric Brain Injury Research Network (PediBIRN) Investigators (2018). Racial and ethnic disparities and bias in the evaluation and reporting of abusive head trauma. *Journal of Pediatrics*. Jul;198:137-143.e1. doi:

10.1016/j.jpeds.2018.0.048. Epub 2018 Mar 29. PMID: 29606408; PMCID: PMC7243470.

Institute of Medicine and National Research Council (2012). Child maltreatment research, policy, and practice for the next decade: Workshop summary. Washington, DC: The National Academies Press. https://doi.org/10.17226/13368.

Krase, K.S. (2013). Differences in racially disproportionate reporting of child maltreatment across report sources. *Journal of Public Child Welfare.*7:4, 351-369, DOI: http://dx.doi.org/10.1080/15548732.2013

Krase, K.S. & Delong Hamilton, T. (2020). *Child welfare: Preparing social workers for practice in the field. New York*: Routledge.

Lau, K., Krase, K., & Morse, R. (2008). *Mandated reporting of child abuse and neglect: A practical guide for social workers.* Springer Publishing Company.

New York State, Office of Children and Family Services, The blind removal process. Administrative Directive, 20-OCFS-ADM-19.

Roberts, D. (2001). *Shattered bonds:The color of child welfare.* Basic-Books: Civitas.

U.S. Department of Health and Human Services, Administration on Children, Youth and Families (2020). *Child Maltreatment 2019* (Washington, DC: U.S. Government Printing Office)

Whitaker, T. R. (2012). Professional social workers in the child welfare workforce: Findings from NASW. *Journal of Family Strengths*: Vol. 12 : Iss. 1 , Article 8. Available at: https://digitalcommons.library.tmc.edu/jfs/vol12/iss1/8.

Wildeman, C., Emanuel, N., Leventhal, J.M., Putnam-Hornstein, E., Waldfogel, J., & Lee, H. (2014). The prevalence of confirmed maltreatment among US children, 2004 to 2011. *Journal of the American Medical Association: Pediatrics.*168(8):706–713. doi:10.1001/jamapediatrics.2014.410

4 |

Identifying Different Types of Child Maltreatment

Child maltreatment is not universally experienced. There are many different types of child maltreatment that professional reporters need to be aware of. And, different types of child maltreatment are more common than others. While we mostly hear about horrific cases of child physical abuse and sexual abuse when they are covered on the news, the reality is that the vast majority of reports made to CPS, and the vast majority of maltreatment experienced by children, involve child neglect. Almost two thirds of total reports to CPS include allegations of neglect only. About 10% of reports include physical abuse allegations only. Fewer than 10% of reports include sexual abuse allegations only. About 15% of reports include multiple types of maltreatment. Medical and healthcare professionals are more likely than other types of mandated reporters to report physical abuse and sexual abuse.

In the previous chapter, we learned that the vast majority of investigations of reports to CPS conclude without determining child maltreatment has occurred. One of the reasons for this is that most reports made to CPS relate to allegations of neglect, and neglect, contrary to physical abuse, isn't something that you can see "proof" of, necessarily. In fact, most "maltreatment" you can't "see" with your eyes. You have to look for the conditions that make it more likely to happen and for the physical or behavioral evidence that it did happen, or is likely to happen. To understand these conditions and what we as professional reporters should be looking for, we will learn about risk factors, indicators, and protective factors.

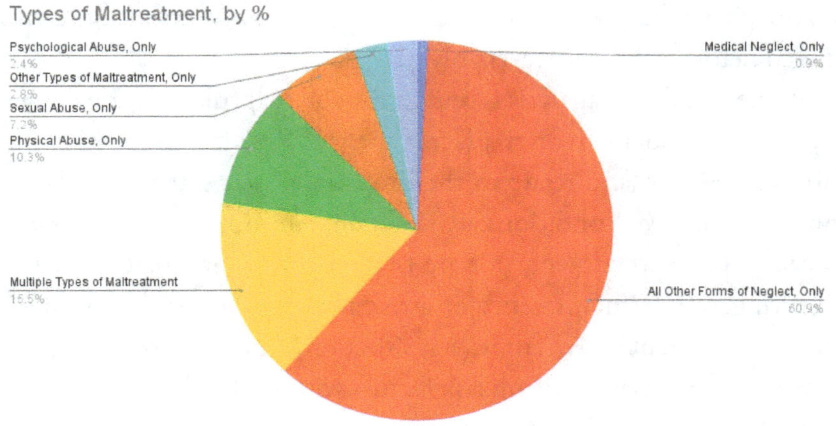

USDHHS, Child Maltreatment, 2019

Risk Factors and Indicators

Risk factors relate to the probability of an undesirable outcome. Risk factors are characteristics or conditions that, if present for a given child, make it more likely that this child, rather than another child, will experience child maltreatment.

Risk factors should be considered along with what we call "indicators." Indicators are evidence of the existence of a particular circumstance or condition; an injury that could have been caused by physical abuse is a physical indicator. A disclosure of abuse or a change in a child's emotional condition is a behavioral indicator. Professional reporters need to consider risk factors and indicators together to determine if the situation before us is likely child maltreatment.

Knowing about risk factors can be really helpful in a world where not all evidence of maltreatment is easily discernible. Knowledge about the risk factors of different types of maltreatment is used to inform development of risk assessments. Risk assessments help determine the potential for maltreatment and the likelihood of recidivism, and they can help systems target resources for intervention of children, families, and communities who need the most help. Ultimately, by intervening where risk factors suggest a high potential for maltreatment, child maltreatment can be prevented before it happens, or intervention can be offered before a child is irreversibly harmed.

While risk factor analysis is important and helpful, there are dangers when we rely too much on risk factor analysis. Risk factors are identified through research and relate to the probability of a statistical relationship between two conditions. Risk factors are not necessarily related to causes of maltreatment, nor are they evidence that maltreatment is occurring. While the presence of a risk factor increases the likelihood that maltreatment will occur in that situation, it does not mean such is a certainty. If we simply rely on risk factors without further discernment, we will falsely identify many cases where, because many risk factors are observed, we think maltreatment is occurring, but it's not; we call these "false positives." When we rely too heavily on risk factor analyses, we also run the risk of ignoring cases in need of intervention because when there are no perceivable risk factors, we assume no maltreatment is occurring, but it is; we call these "false negatives." To avoid false positives and false negatives we need to be comprehensive in our analysis of risk factors.

Research has been used to identify risk factors, in general, for child maltreatment. These risk factors are divided by category: parent and caretaker risk factors, child risk factors, and environmental level/ community risk factors. We will discuss risk factors as they relate to each type of maltreatment later in this chapter.

Parent/Caretaker Risk Factors

- Abused or neglected as a child
- Isolated
- Low self-esteem
- Relationship stress, including abuse
- Physical or mental health problems
  - Including substance use disorders
- Prior perpetration of abuse
- Financial crises/ housing disruption
- Immaturity & unrealistic expectations

Child Risk Factors

- Younger
- Premature infants
- Developmental delays
- Physical/mental disabilities
- Disordered behaviors
- Gender
  - Girls: Higher risk of sexual abuse

Environmental/Community Risk Factors

Community Conditions

- Deficient Services/education system
- Unjust criminal/corrections system
- Local crime

> *Societal Attitudes*
>
> - Acceptance of violence
> - Objectification and sexualization of girls/women

Professional reporters need to be especially aware of the impact that societal attitudes have on child maltreatment. Simply put, when society accepts violence as a means of interaction between adults, it should come as no surprise that the use of violence as a means of interaction with children would also happen. Additionally, when societal attitudes continue to propagate a system where girls and women are routinely objectified and sexualized, it should come as no surprise that girls are more likely to be sexually abused than boys. All members of a society can impact community level risk factors. Knowing about risk factors at the individual, community, and macro levels can help professional reporters determine how to support prevention efforts and responsible interventions.

Risk of Child Maltreatment Fatality

The ultimate goal of the child protection system is to prevent harm to children, with a specific focus on preventing child fatalities. While it is likely impossible to prevent all such deaths, the goal is to get as close as possible to zero child deaths caused by maltreatment. In 2019, between 1,500-1,800 children died as a result of child maltreatment in the United States. This number equates to about 2-3 children out of every 100,000.

Research finds that children who die of child maltreatment usually experience multiple risk factors and that younger children (infants and toddlers) are especially at risk. Boys are more likely than girls to be victims of child fatalities, but we are more likely to hear about the deaths of girls in the news media. And, neglect is associated with over 70% of child fatalities.

In order to prevent child maltreatment fatalities, concerted efforts need to be dedicated to support families, especially those with young children, and to prevent neglect. We will discuss advocacy efforts that can support families with young children in Chapter 8.

Protective Factors

Risk factors are important to know so that society can set up systems to protect children and support families. However, there are other important factors to consider, called "protective factors." Both research and anecdotal information have identified many families with multiple risk factors for child maltreatment, yet the children in the family are not just safe but thriving. How is this possible? What's the secret? If we knew the secret, we could reproduce it and save millions of children from harm, right?

Research has identified five central "protective factors" for child maltreatment: parental resilience, parental knowledge of child development and parenting skills, concrete support for families, social connections, and family cohesion.

Resilience is a catch-all term that is used to explain why good things happen when bad things are expected. Some people are "resilient" and can bounce back after tragedy with strength. There are other people for whom the slightest disruption to their lives can be catastrophic. Parents who easily cope with the stresses of life, or occasional crisis, are considered resilient. Resilient parents have the capacity to navigate tough situations and confidently regain control and calm. When parents face multiple life stressors, such as a history of trauma, health problems, relationship conflict, violence, and financial stress, parents may be less resilient and struggle with meeting the needs of their children.

Parents who know more about child development and develop skills for appropriately intervening to support their child's development are less likely to maltreat their children. Research shows that parents who are loving, responsive to their children's needs, and consistent with expectations and who support their children's age-appropriate independence are less likely to maltreat their children.

Families who have what they need, including access to food, clothing, housing, and transportation are less likely to maltreat their children. Families who can easily access essential services, such as childcare, healthcare, and mental health services to address family-specific needs are even better able to support the well-being of their children.

Parenting is tough. The old adage, "It takes a village to raise a child," is based on thousands of years of cultural experiences. Research consistently shows that families with a support network of extended family members, friends, neighbors, community, etc., have an easier time meeting their children's needs.

Strong emotional ties between children and their caretakers, along with a pattern of positive interaction between the two, is found to protect children from maltreatment. But, which came first? Does the emotional connection and positive interaction reduce the likelihood of maltreatment? Or does a reduced likelihood of maltreatment lead to more of an emotional connection with positive interaction? These are important questions to focus on when aiming to prevent and respond to child maltreatment.

Throughout the rest of this chapter, we will explore different types of maltreatment. For each type of maltreatment, a definition will be provided with context. Specific indicators and risk factors for each type of maltreatment will be highlighted. We will use case examples to clarify the nuances related to identifying each type of maltreatment. Ultimately, we will use knowledge of types of maltreatment to inform the application of the framework to decide whether to make a report, outlined in Chapter 5.

Child Neglect

What is Neglect?

Child neglect is most frequently defined as the failure of a parent or other person with responsibility for the child to provide needed food, clothing, shelter, medical care, or supervision to the degree that the child's health, safety, and well-being are threatened with harm.

More generally, neglect can be explained as parental failure to meet a child's basic needs. This type of neglect is often referred to as "physical neglect." Neglect, more broadly, can also include parental failure to provide an adequate level of care in specific areas, like supervision, education, or medical attention.

Neglect is often differentiated from other forms of maltreatment in that neglect usually involves omission, rather than commission; this means parents might be considered neglectful because they HAVEN'T done something, instead of HAVING done something. Because neglect is often related to an omission, there might be no physical evidence of maltreatment.

What are the Consequences of Neglect?

The consequences of neglect on children can be physical, including injury or illness. The consequences of neglect on children can also be mental or emotional. Physical consequences are easier to observe and report. Mental and emotional consequences are more difficult to appraise.

Reports of Neglect

The original framers of mandated reporting policy did NOT want to mandate the reporting of suspicions of neglect. They wanted the legal requirement to report suspicions of maltreatment to be limited to physical and sexual abuse. Since the definitions of neglect are very subjective, they feared a high number of reports of neglect, with a low rate of substantiation upon investigation. Unfortunately, the advice of these experts was not heeded.

The vast majority of reports to CPS involve concerns of neglect. About 60% of reports to CPS involve only an allegation of neglect. When including reports with multiple allegation types, more than 2/3 of reports include neglect concerns.

Research finds that reporters are most unsure about making reports of neglect. Therefore, it is not surprising that reports of neglect are the least likely to be supported by evidence during a CPS investigation.

Parental Intent

When considering if your concerns for a child rise to the definition of neglect, there are some key things to consider. For instance, what is the intent of the parent? Is the parent trying to do something right or good, but they are challenged by particular conditions that they have or don't have control over? Then it might not be neglectful. If the parent doesn't seem to care about the impact of the situation on the child, then it is more likely neglectful.

How is Poverty Related to Neglect?

When considering whether a parent is responsible for neglect, a reporter needs to consider whether poverty is the presenting issue. There is a strong link between family poverty and child neglect, but we need to be careful to not be deeming parents neglectful just because the family lives in poverty. Families living in poverty experience higher levels of stress than other families, and thus are at higher risk of neglect. They are also more likely to be reported to CPS than other families, due in part to their increased access to or visibility by mandated reporters. And, then there's the reality that many judge families living in poverty as failures.

When reporters view parents as failing, it might make it easier for them to feel comfortable reporting them to CPS.

The law is pretty clear: poverty, alone, is not child maltreatment. Luckily, we have some societal systems in place that aim to mitigate the harmful impacts of poverty on children. Reporters should be ready to utilize those systems to help children and their families. It can be argued that professional reporters have a moral obligation to support such systems, and any other effort that makes it less likely that children and families will find themselves in poverty. But, for starters, if a parent is financially unable to provide for the child, it is incumbent upon the reporter, and society at large, to help the family access services necessary to provide for the child. Punishing the parent and child for living in poverty is not helpful.

Risk of Neglect

We have talked about risk in the context of "risk factors." As we address each type of maltreatment, we will also discuss risk of maltreatment. If the child hasn't been negatively impacted by their caretaker's behavior yet, it could still be considered neglect. However, if harm to the child hasn't been realized yet, it is also still possible to prevent such harm.

Therefore, it is important for professional reporters to think about how to help prevent harm to children. In Chapter 5, we will consider the risk of harm to the child in a given situation and whether the risk can be mitigated by the professional reporter without a call to CPS.

Physical Neglect

The most basic form of neglect the law acknowledges is physical neglect. Physical neglect is when a parent fails to provide adequate food, shelter, or clothing for a child. "Adequate" is the key word in the definition. Adequacy can, however, be subjective.

Food

Inadequate food is a complicated situation. It is NOT neglect when a child is not given the food they want or when the quality of the food they are given is not what you, the reporter, would like to provide to your child. Children who show up at school hungry reporting that they haven't eaten breakfast are not necessarily neglected. Food insecurity is a major societal problem in the United States. Thankfully, most schools provide free and reduced cost breakfast and lunch to children who need it. The federal government provides food support through programs like WIC (Women Infants and Children) and the Supplemental Nutritional Assistance Program (aka "SNAP," formerly known as "food stamps"). There are additional food related services available in many communities, including food bank services. A determination of neglect would not be made simply because a child is hungry. Before CPS can make a finding of neglect for inadequate food, they would assess if the parent is trying to meet the child's needs. Ideally, a reporter could help support the parent in meeting those needs.

Shelter/Housing

Inadequate shelter is also a complicated issue. It is NOT neglect when a child shares a bed with a sibling or sleeps on the floor in a small apartment. These arrangements are not ideal, but as long as the place is safe, it is adequate.

It is NOT neglect just because there are roaches, mice, or even rats in a child's home. The existence of these pests in the home may signal neglect if the parent is not doing what they can to make the living situation better. But, especially in housing complexes with multiple dwellings, the existence of vermin is beyond the control of a single resident.

Homeless children are not automatically considered neglected, either. Living out of a car or on the streets can be dangerous for a child, even if in the care of a parent. Situations like this can put children at risk for illness and violence. However, the cost of housing is prohibitively expensive for many low income families, and the availability of resources to assist families in finding affordable housing varies greatly by community. If a parent refuses assistance, or is not making efforts to better the child's living conditions, they are likely to be deemed as failing to meet their child's shelter needs.

Many inadequate shelter cases with CPS involvement are what is often referred to as "dirty house" cases. In dirty house cases, parents are often struggling with mental health and/or substance use disorders that resultingly make it impossible for them to manage their home environment. These cases might involve hoarding and/or unclean living conditions that threaten the health and safety of any child in the home.

Clothing

Parents are expected to appropriately clothe their children. This, generally, means that children should be dressed in clothing appropriate for the weather and that the clothing be clean. Children grow quickly, and clothing is expensive. In cases where a child is wearing old shoes or clothing that is inappropriately sized, it is important for a reporter to first determine if the clothing is adequate to meet the child's basic needs and whether the parent's intent is to take care of the child. In cases where a child could use newer, or more appropriately sized clothing, but it is clear that the parents are trying their best under the circumstances, it would be most helpful for a reporter to assist the family in identifying a program where they could receive donations of clothing.

It is NOT neglect just because a child is wearing old clothes, but it might be neglect if they are consistently wearing dirty or smelly clothing. The important issue to note in these situations is the parent's intent. If the parent is trying to keep the child clean and well cared for, it is not neglect. For instance, some kids refuse to be bathed or demand that they wear their favorite clothes day, after day, after day... I've known 4- or 5-year-olds who refuse to change out of their favorite dress for a week... *that 4- or 5-year-old might have been me.*

> *Consider This Case*
>
> *A 9-year-old child has a cold with a fever. After a few days, they develop a sinus infection. The parents seek medical intervention. During intake, you are told that the child was sent to school while they had a fever in order to receive breakfast and lunch through the school meal program. You also find out that the child rarely is served dinner at night. Is this neglect? If so, what kind?*
>
> Well, maybe. The child was sent to school sick. That's problematic. The child has limited food in the home. That's problematic too. But, was the child harmed? We're not sure, but there is certainly a risk of harm. What was the parent's intent? Was the parent clueless to the child's condition? Doesn't seem like it. It looks like they sent their child to school in order for the child to be fed. Maybe the parent had to go to work, and they don't have paid sick days. Maybe they were concerned about leaving the child home alone. The parents might have made a tough choice to keep their child safe. It is possible that this is physical neglect. We will discuss this case again in Chapter 5, when we explore the framework to help us consider the decision to make a call to CPS, or not.

Educational Neglect

Educational neglect is generally defined as the failure to enroll a child of mandatory school age in school or provide appropriate home schooling, ignoring special education needs, or permitting chronic school absenteeism. Not all states have educational neglect clearly defined in their law. But, all states have a law around "compulsory education."

The age at which children are required to attend school varies by state. To find out the ages for compulsory school attendance in your state, conduct an internet search for: "age of compulsory school attendance in [your state]".

Most generally, kids are required to be "enrolled" in school (or be receiving approved home schooling) from ages 5 or 6 to 16-18. For instance, in New York State compulsory education laws require kids to be enrolled in school from 6-16 (17 in NYC). In that state, kids of kindergarten age don't have to go to school, and once a kid turns 16, they can't be forced to go to school by the government unless their parents want them to.

The ages for compulsory education laws are largely based on expectations for parenting. Kids aren't all required to attend school at age 3 because society, generally, still expects parents, usually mothers, to be taking care of young kids in the home even though the reality is that most moms work outside of the home. About half of states require students to stay in school until they are 18 or 19, or they have graduated from high school. That means almost half of states DO NOT require students to stay in school that long. When compulsory education laws were first passed in the beginning of the 20th century, older teenagers (16–19-year-olds) were often important wage earners in a household. So, the laws were originally designed to allow children to leave their educational pursuits in order to go to work for the security of their family. While times have changed and the employment systems prefer workers with at least a high school education, the laws in many states have not changed to require students to stay in school until they turn 18 or graduate from high school.

Educational neglect is a concern for CPS because children who do not get access to education might fail to acquire basic life skills or knowledge necessary to succeed. For children with special education needs, schools are often the conduit through which they receive services to support their physical health or emotional growth and development,

The law in all states provides parents with the right to make educational decisions about their child. So "educational neglect" can be a tricky subject. If a parent doesn't like what a school is teaching their child, they can't force the school to teach what they want, but they can pick another school or homeschool their child (as long as they follow the homeschooling law in their state). When a group of parents doesn't like what a public school in their community is teaching, or not teaching, their kids, they may use political power to influence school policy or curricula. We see this debate often in terms of the relationships between religious beliefs and public school science curricula.

Educational neglect cases that come to the attention of CPS most often include situations related to parental or child physical illness, mental illness, or substance use disorder. In these cases, a parent might not be able to support their child's successful involvement in their own schooling. Oftentimes these situations are situational, or short term, when the family is under particularly high levels of stress.

Some concerns for educational neglect relate to children, usually adolescents, who avoid attending school because of social or behavioral problems at school, including bullying or violence. It is important for schools to be active in evaluating situations where a child does not feel safe and provide interventions to address their safety and concerns.

Other reports of educational neglect might relate to situations where a school has been attempting to engage a parent to help solve a problem for the child, but the parent is resistant to the school's efforts. There are situations where the school wants to evaluate a child for special education, or other supportive services, but the parent refuses. Parents may refuse because they don't want their child to be labelled, or the parents deny the child is having difficulty. There are other situations where services are recommended for a child, but the parent refuses to consent to those services. These are not easy situations for schools to navigate. Ultimately, parents have the right to make educational decisions for their child, but schools are charged with evaluating the child's needs and providing the appropriate services. Ideally, the relationship between schools and parents would be collaborative, and many of these tense situations could be avoided. But, not every situation is ideal.

In some states, like New York, the law requires schools to make significant efforts to mitigate educational neglect concerns before making a call, or CPS is held to a higher standard of mitigating consequences before filing a case against a parent for educational neglect in Family Court. In cases where the parents genuinely care about the child's education and health, it would be ideal to find a way to get the school and the family on the same page so that the child is afforded every opportunity possible.

> ### Consider This Case
>
> *A 14-year-old student has 15 nonconsecutive absences from school by October. Is this educational neglect?*
>
> In some jurisdictions, this level of absence would have automatically triggered an investigation, at least by the school, if not yet a call to CPS. But, we don't know what is going on. Perhaps there was a death in the family or a significant illness. Perhaps the parents have no idea the child is missing school. These are all questions that the school should have answers to before asking CPS to intervene with an investigation of educational neglect.

Medical Neglect

Medical neglect is defined as the failure of parents to provide adequate and appropriate medical care to a child. Medical care generally includes physical healthcare, dental care, optometric/vision care, etc. Medical care is expensive. Therefore, the inability of a parent to provide medical care due to poverty is generally not legally considered medical neglect. Parents might, instead, need assistance getting their children the medical care they need but the family can't afford.

Every state has a "Child Health Insurance Program"/ CHIP, which provides no- or low-cost child health insurance as well as dental and vision coverage. This insurance is guaranteed at the federal level, but it is only available to American citizens and certain legal residents of the country. If a child is not receiving the medical care they need because the family does not realize the child is eligible for insurance coverage, you can refer the family to your state's Child Health Insurance Program. If the child is not eligible for CHIP, there might be other low- or no-cost options available in the community.

Parents who refuse to allow their child's medical condition to be treated because of religious beliefs are not committing medical neglect. The United States Constitution protects the right to religious expression, and parents have the right to dictate their children's religious expression until the child becomes an adult. However, in cases where a parental refusal to accept treatment for a child's medical condition would create a significant risk to a child's life, healthcare providers can seek assistance from the state in mandating such treatment. For instance, when parents have religious beliefs that include refusal of blood transfusions or organ transplants, but a child's life is at risk without such transfusion or transplant, the state will step in and consent to the treatment against the parents' wishes. In this situation the state is using its "Parens Patriae" power (i.e., the government as the legal protector of citizens unable to protect themselves) to act as parent for the child.

> ### *Consider This Case*
>
> *A 7 year old child is under the care of a pulmonologist at a community-based health clinic affiliated with the local hospital, due to a history of asthma. Two months ago, the child was prescribed an inhaled corticosteroid by the clinic physician. They were due for a follow-up visit a few weeks ago to evaluate their progress under this treatment plan. The family did not show for the appointment. An attempt was made to reschedule the follow-up visit, without success. A month after missing the appointment, the child presents at the local hospital's emergency department suffering from an acute asthma*

attack. The parents explain they ran out of the inhaled corticosteroid, and the short-acting beta2-agonist was not sufficiently controlling the episode.

Cases of medical neglect are most often found when healthcare providers feel that parents are not taking seriously a child's chronic health condition; the child might miss important appointments or fail to follow medication protocols that put the child's health at risk. In some cases the parents might not understand the importance of the provider's plan for the child's healthcare, or the parent might not understand what the plan entails. It may be that missed appointments are due to complications in parental work schedules or the challenges of navigating life as a single parent. And, failure to follow medication protocols may have more to do with the cost of prescription medications than unwillingness to follow the plan.

While the child's current asthma attack could be related to the failure to continue the medication protocol, it is also possible that the child would have had the attack even if they were still taking the medication. The healthcare provider could work with the family to determine a plan to better adhere to the treatment plan and follow-up visits (perhaps using a combination of in-person and tele-health sessions). A report to CPS won't necessarily help get the child the care they need, and might make it less likely the family will be comfortable communicating with the healthcare provider when they need help in the future.

Inadequate Supervision

Any parent knows the feeling of wondering at what age it is all right to leave their child home alone, and for how long. Inadequate supervision, as a form of child neglect and maltreatment, is when a parent leaves a child alone when they shouldn't or when they leave the child with an inappropriate caretaker or in an unsafe situation. Sometimes inadequate supervision has nothing to do with leaving the child alone, but rather failing to appropriately monitor the child, allowing them to engage in risky or harmful behaviors.

In some states, the law defines a specific age a child can be left alone, for example 8, 10, or 12, and for how long a child can be left alone, for example one hour or five hours. Most states do not have a law that specifies an age. Since most states do not have a law that specifies parameters, parents in those states have the right to make a decision about what is best for their child and family, as long as the child is safe and well cared for. For some families, this means that an 8-year-old can safely stay home while their parent goes to the store, or a 12-year-old can watch a younger sibling while their parent goes out to dinner. In other families, this might mean that a particular 16-year-old who can't quite be trusted yet shouldn't be left home alone... at ... all.

To determine if leaving a child unsupervised necessitates a call to child protective services, consider the age of the child, the maturity of the child, the safety of the child, and the intent of the parent. If the parent is not considering the needs and guarding the safety of the child when leaving the child alone or not supervising them, the situation may necessitate CPS intervention. However, if a parent leaves a child home alone at an age or for a duration that you would not feel comfortable doing with your own child, you should stop and consider if you are judging the parent or making an informed decision. We will discuss this more in Chapter 5.

When a parent has left a child unsupervised without the intention of coming back or without a plan to care for the child in the future, this is abandonment. Abandonment is always reportable to CPS. In some cases abandonment is also a crime. The American Infant Protection Act shelters parents from criminal responsibility if they safely abandon a young child in an appropriate place, like a hospital, police precinct, or firehouse. The goal of this law is to encourage parents who are considering abandoning their children to do so safely, and not risk the child's life in the process. The abandonment would still result in a report to CPS.

There are many issues that contribute to reports of inadequate supervision, and many are not related to what many would consider "bad parenting." Many inadequate supervision cases involve parental mental illness or substance use disorders. However, there are also many parents who leave their children unsupervised when they wish they had another choice. Childcare is expensive, and work schedules can be grueling. We, unfortunately, hear too many stories of children who get injured because they are left alone while a parent goes to work, and childcare isn't available.

There are many ways to reduce risk of inadequate supervision, including affordable childcare and universal paid sick leave laws. Another option includes widespread awareness campaigns that aim to educate parents so that children who are left alone are done so with the resources they need to in order to be safe.

Consider This Case

A 10-year-old is left home alone for 9 hours on a weekend while their parent is at work.

In some states, like Illinois, this would be against the law. But, is the child being neglected? What about the parent's level of care? Is the child safe? Do they have the maturity or preparation for the situation? We will explore this case in Chapter 5.

Physical Abuse

Child physical abuse is defined as when someone legally responsible for a child inflicts, or allows to be inflicted, what the law considers injury to a child. "Injury" can include everything from a simple bruise or scrape to a cut, burn, or broken bone. While a bruise may not seem like a serious injury, a bruise is a physical indicator of internal injury and bleeding. The law related to physical abuse often relates behaviors that cause injury to children, such as striking, kicking burning, or biting the child to physical abuse.

The definition of child physical abuse also includes situations when the responsible person creates, or allows to be created, substantial risk of injury to a child. In such a case, the child does not have to be injured for a parent to be found responsible for physical abuse. It is enough that the parent's actions, or failure to act, created a risk due to which the child could have been physically injured.

The easiest way to consider whether an action of a parent which leads to a child's injury, or creates a risk of injury to the child, is physical abuse is to consider intent: did the parent mean to hurt the child with their action? Did the parent take an action without regard for the risk to the child? Or was the action an accident?

If a parent, enraged with anger, hits a child in the head with a base-ball bat causing an injury, this is clearly child abuse. If a parent becomes so enraged that they attempt to hit the child in the head with the bat, but the child avoids contact, this is still child abuse because the parent's actions have created a substantial risk of injury, even if the child is physically unharmed.

However, if the parent is swinging the bat while playing a game, and the child moves into the path of the moving bat, and the parent doesn't realize until too late that the child is in jeopardy and hits the child causing injury, that's NOT physical abuse; it is an accident.

The location of the injury might give you a clue as to whether the injury was accidental or intentional. When children, or adults for that matter, fall in an accident, they tend to hurt themselves in particular areas, including their elbows, their knees, or their shins. It is harder for children to hurt themselves on their backside, especially from their buttocks and down their legs. The buttocks are generally a cushion to a fall on and unlikely to bruise without serious force (though a hard fall could do it). It is really hard to bruise the backs of your legs, since someone falling backwards will usually fall on their buttocks or brace their fall by putting their arms behind them. Therefore, it is important to consider the part of the body that is injured, in context with the explanation for an injury, when trying to determine if the cause was abuse.

Corporal Punishment

Many people ask: if hitting a child can be physical abuse, then isn't spanking, and other forms of corporal punishment, physical abuse? Distinguishing corporal punishment from physical abuse can be complicated, but here are some important points to understand.

Corporal punishment is defined as the use of physical force in disciplining a child. An important part of the definition is "discipline." The parent takes the action with the intent of punishing a child for a behavior the parent did not like, often in the hopes of preventing the child from turning to that sort of behavior in the future. Corporal punishment commonly includes spanking a child on the buttocks or slapping a child on the hand. Corporal punishment can also include having a child endure physical discomfort and pain, such as kneeling on rice, squatting with their back on a wall, or standing with their arms suspended from their sides. Corporal punishment can include "washing a child's mouth out with soap" or forcing the child to ingest hot sauce or hot pepper flakes. Corporal punishment is common in some communities and less common in others. Contrary to the belief of many, corporal punishment is permissible by parents in all states in the United States.

Corporal punishment is NOT automatically considered physical abuse. If corporal punishment causes injury, including a bruise, scrape, or cut, it IS physical abuse. If the punishment is such that it creates a substantial risk of injury, it is also physical abuse.

For this reason, a parent slapping a child across the face is generally considered physical abuse. The risk of injuring a child's mouth, nose, or eyes or causing a head injury is very high with contact to the area. Also, the use of an implement, like a belt or cord, especially on bare skin, makes the risk of injury high, and therefore is generally considered physical abuse.

Threats of corporal punishment are not considered abuse. When corporal punishment does not cause physical injury, nor create a substantial risk of injury, it might still be considered child maltreatment as "excessive." Excessive corporal punishment is considered neglect in many states. Corporal punishment might be deemed excessive if:

- The intent of the parent's actions is to scare the child, and not discipline them; or
- The frequency, nature and severity, appropriateness, or duration of the punishment seems excessive.

For instance, if the punishment happens very often, it would suggest that as a form of discipline it is not working. If a child accidentally spills their drink, but gets spanked, this might be excessive. Corporal punishment is unlikely to help prevent accidents, and in fact, the fear of corporal punishment is more likely to create stress in a child that leads to lack of physical control over their body.

If, as a mandated reporter, you learn about the use of corporal punishment that hasn't caused injury, and the family in question might not understand the law in your state, you might want to provide them with resources to help them understand alternative forms of discipline or, at least, help them understand when corporal punishment might be deemed abuse.

Indicators of Physical Abuse

Physical indicators of possible physical abuse include:

- Broken bones (i.e., fractures)
- Burns
- Cuts (i.e., lacerations)
- Head injuries
- Scalp injuries
- Bruises/welts
- Induced injury, where parents create a situation to make their child unwell, as in the case of Munchausen by Proxy Syndrome

Behavioral indicators of possible physical abuse include:

- Social anxiety
- Aggression/bullying
- Chronic running away
- Fear of going home
- Self-blame
- Hiding injuries
- Depression

While these physical and behavioral indicators may suggest physical abuse, just because any of these indicators is present does NOT mean that physical abuse is definitely occurring. Bruises and welts can be caused by other actions or accidents. Bite marks might be from altercations with children, which, while unfortunate, do not suggest a parental failure. Burns, fractures, and head injuries can also occur by accident. Behavioral indicators can be the result of non-abusive situations. It is important to understand these injuries and indicators in context.

Consequences of Physical Abuse

Physical abuse can lead to many physical, behavioral, or psychological conditions.

For instance, physical abuse can cause medical or neurological conditions, including shaken-baby syndrome. Cognitive, behavioral, psychosocial/psychiatric, and socio-emotional difficulties can result from physical abuse, including future substance abuse and physically abusive behaviors. Some of these difficulties might be due to anxiety or stress caused by childhood physical abuse, but some of these resulting conditions could come from traumatic brain injury caused by the abuse.

We are learning a lot about the impact of head injury in children on their development of certain conditions later in life. We see how repeated head trauma causes chronic traumatic encephalopathy (CTE) in football players, for instance. We barely know the extent to which minor head trauma in children can lead to behavioral and cognitive problems later in life.

Risk Factors for Physical Abuse

There are many issues that contribute to the likelihood of physical abuse in one family, as opposed to another family, like stress. Families living in poverty, those who have a child with special needs, and families where the adult caretakers are having relationship problems, including abuse, all have high levels of stress. That stress can lead to frustrations and anger that are misplaced against children through abusive behaviors. Additionally, when there is parental mental illness or substance use disorders, physical abuse is more likely. Parents with a history of prior victimization as a child are also more likely to victimize their children, thus creating what is called a "cycle of abuse." However, that cycle CAN be broken through awareness and support.

Consider This Case

A 6-year-old child presents to a pediatric urgent care center for evaluation of a possible wrist fracture. They also have bruises on their cheek, upper arm, and torso. The child and their parent, independently, tell you the child fell down the stairs. They both, independently, tell you the child is a "klutz".

Is the child being physically abused?

Kids fall, but when kids with normal physical development fall, they usually fall forward, scraping their knees or falling on their hands, or fall backward onto their hands, elbows, or buttocks.

All the areas in which this child is injured are in areas the body would responsively protect (i.e., face, upper arm, and torso). If, however, your familiarity with this child, or your gut feeling communicating with the child and parent, suggests the child is very rambunctious and falls a lot in odd ways, then you would likely conclude this is just accidental injury. But if you feel like it is more likely these injuries were inflicted on the child, you would need to consider contacting CPS.

Consider This Case

An 8-year-old child plays a prank on their grandmother which is considered disrespectful in the family's culture. The punishment is that the child must keep their arms up over their head for many minutes.

> Is this physical abuse? Is there injury? Is there a significant risk of injury? Not really.
>
> It IS corporal punishment, but is it excessive? The punishment does not seem outsized to the infraction. We'd need to know about the frequency and duration.
>
> What we know so far does not suggest the punishment is excessive. Research suggests the use of corporal punishment is unlikely to deter undesirable future behavior from children. It might be helpful to explain to the family other options for discipline or to help them understand that if the child is injured in the future, this would be considered abuse.

Sexual Abuse

There are approximately half a million cases of child sexual abuse each year in the United States. Research suggests that one in five girls will be abused by the age of 18 and that one in ten boys will be abused by the age of 18. It is also understood that these numbers might be undercounted. It is important to note that child sexual abuse is not about "stranger danger." In fact, 90% of children are abused by someone they know.

Child sexual abuse can be defined, most broadly, as engaging children in sexual activities. While sexualized behavior by children is a normal part of their development, it is important to note that a child cannot legally consent to sexual activity with others until they reach a particular age. This age of consent varies by state, but generally ranges from 16-18. (For a list of age of consent by state: https://aspe.hhs.gov/reports/statutory-rape-guide-state-laws-reporting-requirements-1)

When children under the age of consent have what would be considered consensual sexual relations with other children under the age of consent, this behavior is not considered child sexual abuse because both parties are children. If an adult has sexual relations with a child under the age of consent, this is a crime and can also be considered child sexual abuse when perpetrated by a parent or other person legally responsible for the child's care. A defense that the child under the age of consent was a willing participant is invalid since children cannot consent to sexual activity.

Sexual abuse includes touching and non-touching actions that are classified through their purpose of sexual gratification, usually of the perpetrator. Sexual abuse includes rape, statutory rape, molestation, prostitution, child pornography, and other forms of sexual exploitation of children or incest with children. Any act that forces, coerces, or threatens a child to have any form of sexual contact or to engage in any type of sexual activity at the perpetrator's discretion is sexual abuse.

A person legally responsible for a child who conducts this behavior is considered a perpetrator and thus responsible for their actions. If the person who conducts this behavior is NOT a person legally responsible for the child, but a person who is legally responsible for the child allows this conduct to occur, they are both responsible for sexual abuse. All forms of child sexual abuse are crimes as well as reportable to CPS.

Indicators of Child Sexual Abuse

It is important to remember that some indicators of child sexual abuse can also be explained by other, non-abusive situations.

Physical indicators of child sexual abuse include:

- Difficulty in walking or sitting
- Torn, stained, or bloody underclothing
- Pain, itching, bruises, or bleeding in genital areas
- Bruises to the hard or soft palate
- Sexually transmitted diseases, especially in preteens

- Pregnancy, especially in the early adolescent years
- Painful discharge of urine and/or repeated urinary infections
- Foreign bodies in vagina or rectum

If you are a reporter in non-medical settings, it might NOT be appropriate for you to assess a child for some of the physical indicators listed.

Behavioral indicators of child sexual abuse include:

- Withdrawal, fantasy, or infantile behavior
- Bizarre, sophisticated, unusual sexual behavior or knowledge
- Seductive or promiscuous behavior
- Extreme fear of being touched/ unwillingness to submit to physical examination
- REPORT OF ABUSE

Responding to a Disclosure of Child Sexual Abuse

If a child discloses to you that they have been sexually abused, it is important to be very careful in how you respond. You should avoid talking about the abuse with the child. Do not ask questions. Do not investigate or interrogate anyone. Allow an investigative team to interview the child. This highly trained unit will use methods that are proven to elicit truthful information from children who have been abused. Please note that it is very common for a child who discloses sexual abuse to recant, or later deny that the abuse happened.

To support a helpful investigation of child sexual abuse make sure you remain calm, listen, and reassure the child that you are there for them and are an advocate for them. Do not overreact, make judgements, make promises that everything will be okay, or tell the child that they will never see the perpetrator again.

We will discuss later when and how to report your suspicions to child protective services.

Risk Factors of Child Sexual Abuse

There are many risk factors for sexual abuse. However, remember that there are plenty of families who live with these risk factors and do not experience sexual abuse, and then there are families with no risk factors for whom sexual abuse is endemic.

Risk factors for victims of child sexual abuse include:

- Prior victimization of the child and/or siblings
- Parental history of child abuse victimization
- Parental problems including violence in the relationship
- Low quality of parent-child relation
- Having a stepfather
- Social isolation of child and/or family
- Child having a mental/physical chronic condition
- Female child
- Child who identifies as LGBTQ+
- Low family support
- Absent or single parent
- Parental substance abuse
- Poverty
- Low level of parental education
- Impulsive child
- Emotional child
- Adolescence

Risk factors of perpetrators include:

- Prior victimization or perpetration of child sexual abuse
- Sexually abusive role models
- Coercive sexual fantasies
- General aggressiveness and acceptance of violence
- Social isolation/poor social skills
- Alcoholism/substance abuse
- Low self-esteem
- Emotionally unsupportive and physically violent family environment
- Association with sexually aggressive, hyper-masculine, and delinquent peers

At a societal level, the culture of male dominance, hyper-valuing male sexuality, and denigrating female roles contributes to the acceptance and continuation of sexual abuse, especially with children.

Under-reporting of Child Sexual Abuse

Child sexual abuse allegations only make up 10% of all reports to CPS in a given year. We know based on other research that sexual abuse is vastly underreported. Why is child sexual abuse so underreported?

Unlike most forms of physical abuse, most forms of sexual abuse (mainly non-penetrative forms of abuse) provide little to no risk of physical indicators. While there are many behavioral indicators identified through research, many of these indicators can be responses to other experiences, including normal development, traumatic experiences, or stress.

Additionally, children often don't report their victimization. Sexual abuse perpetrators often groom children so that children are less likely to report the behavior. Child victims might be told they are special. Or they might be told that they did something wrong and that they will get in trouble if they tell.

It is also difficult for reporters to differentiate normal sexualized behavior from indicators of abuse. Sexual behavior is not often discussed in "polite company," and, therefore, even professional reporters might be uncomfortable with the topic and thus avoid it, especially when working with children.

And lastly, we, as a society, do a horrible job at protecting people, especially girls, from sexualized violence. A lot more needs to be done to protect children from sexual abuse.

Consider This Case

You overhear a six-year old child offering to show a similarly aged child their "privates," if they show theirs. When the other child refuse, the child tries to pull down the other child's pants.

Is this behavior indicative of sexual abuse? Unlikely. Kids are natural explorers; it is normal for them to be interested in body parts and whether other kids have the same parts they do. However, it is NOT okay for kids to pull down each other's pants.

For some people, it might seem natural to laugh at this behavior, but it's not a good idea to condone or reward this kind of behavior by being amused. There needs to be a serious, but non-threatening, discussion here about privacy and consent. Even the youngest children can learn that their body is their own. Ideally, children should feel confident in the agency over their own body and respect the agency of others.

> **Consider This Case**
>
> *A 5-year-old presents to their regular pediatrician's office with painful and reluctant urination. Urinalysis confirms a urinary tract infection. While waiting for the examination the child seems physically uncomfortable. A physical examination finds the child extremely protective of their body. When you inquire if they are ok, they say that someone hurt them "down there".*
>
> At this point, you have physical and behavioral indicators of sexual abuse. Unless you are trained in the evaluation of child sexual abuse, it is very important to allow experts in the subject area to continue any conversation about how the child developed their symptoms. A report to CPS should be made immediately, which may result in intervention from law enforcement.
>
> You should, however, continue to treat the child's physical condition, so that they can be more comfortable.

Emotional Abuse

Emotional abuse, otherwise known as psychological abuse or maltreatment, is broadly defined as injury to the child's psychological capacity or emotional stability. Emotional abuse includes a pattern of behavior that might involve belittling, ridiculing, intimidating, and/or ignoring/rejecting a child. This type of maltreatment could be characterized as withholding love or seeming unconcerned. Emotional abuse is often found in cases where physical and/or sexual abuse is also occurring.

All indicators of emotional abuse are behavioral. Emotional abuse can result in observable and substantial change in a child's behavior, emotional response, or cognition. Emotional abuse can seriously interfere with a child's positive development. Just like responding to behavioral indicators for other types of maltreatment, it is difficult to determine if the indicators are related to the emotional abuse or some other non-abusive factor in the child's life.

Many parents teeter on the edge of emotional abuse when dealing with their children. Parenting can be frustrating, and it is, unfortunately, very easy to take out frustrations on children. We need to do more to help parents understand that it is normal to be frustrated, or even angered, by kids and their behavior. However, making fun of kids, or calling them names, or being mean just doesn't help; it hurts, more than kids can let grown-ups know.

Consider This Case

During a camp-related physical examination, a parent reports that their very shy and sensitive 7-year-old has trouble getting along with other children. You ask the parent how the child is at home. The parent tells you the child is "stuck-up," and it's no wonder the other children don't like them. You overhear the parent ridiculing the child in the parking lot as they leave the office, telling the child they are worthless and stupid.

There's no other way to put this. This is bad parenting. It likely meets the definition of emotional abuse. Unfortunately, the parents might not realize the impact that this behavior has on kids. The parents might have been treated like this as children, themselves.

The big question we're left with is whether to make a report or not. In the next chapter we will examine a framework to help us make the tough call – whether to make a report to CPS, or not.

Test Questions

A 14-year-old child doesn't come home after school. They return home after midnight obviously drunk. Their distraught parent slaps them across the face. Which of the following forms of child maltreatment might have occurred?

a. Neglect
b. Physical Abuse
c. Sexual Abuse
d. Emotional Abuse
e. Medical Neglect

A 9-year-old child has a cold with a fever. The parent keeps them home from school, as per school policy. The parent leaves the child unattended for 9 hours while they go to work. Which of the following forms of child maltreatment might be happening?

a. Physical Neglect
b. Educational Neglect
c. Medical Neglect
d. Inadequate Supervision

A 9-year-old child has a cold with a persistent cough. The parent brings the child to the doctor, and the doctor diagnoses the child with asthma and schedules a follow-up visit. The child does not show to the follow-up visit. Which of the following forms of child maltreatment might be happening?

a. Physical Neglect
b. Educational Neglect
c. Medical Neglect
d. Inadequate Supervision

A 12-year-old child has not attended school in three weeks, and the parents have not responded to attempts to communicate from the school. Which of the following forms of child maltreatment might be happening?

a. Physical Neglect
b. Educational Neglect
c. Medical Neglect
d. Inadequate Supervision

A 15-year-old girl tells her friend that she is having sex with her mother's new boyfriend. Which of the following forms of child maltreatment might have happened?

a. Neglect
b. Physical Abuse
c. Sexual Abuse
d. Emotional Abuse
e. Medical Neglect

Discussion Questions

- What are your personal experiences with the use of corporal punishment? What are your personal beliefs about whether corporal punishment is an appropriate method of discipline for children?
- Considering the risk factor research, what can society do better, or more of, to prevent child maltreatment?

Resources

For more information on the physical and behavioral indicators of child maltreatment, utilize these reputable resources:

- Recognizing Child Abuse and Neglect: Signs and Symptoms, Child Welfare Information Gateway, https://www.childwelfare.gov/pubPDFs/signs.pdf
- Child Abuse, Mayo Clinic https://www.mayoclinic.org/diseases-conditions/child-abuse/symptoms-causes/syc-20370864

References

Austin AE, Lesak AM, Shanahan ME. (2020). Risk and protective factors for child maltreatment: A review. *Current Epidemiology Reports*. 7(4):334-342. doi: 10.1007/s40471-020-00252-3. PMID: 34141519; PMCID: PMC8205446.

Besharov, D. J. (1990). *Recognizing child abuse: A guide for the concerned*. Free Press.

Child Welfare Information Gateway, United States Department of Health and Human Services (2020). Definitions of child abuse and neglect, https://www.childwelfare.gov/pubPDFs/define.pdf

Child Welfare Information Gateway, United States Department of Health and Human Services. (2018). Acts of omission: An overview of child neglect, https://www.childwelfare.gov/pubPDFs/acts.pdf

5

Framework for Making the Tough Call: Decision-Making

The question I get most often when training professional reporters on their legal and ethical obligations is: "Do I have to make a report, if...?"

I can never tell someone to make a report or absolve them from responsibility for choosing not to. What I aim to do is provide professional reporters with knowledge and helpful guidance that support a greater understanding of their role so that they can be confident in their own decision to make a report... or not.

Gathering Important Information About Reporting in Your State

In this chapter, we will outline a framework you can use when trying to make the decision whether to make a call to CPS, or not. In order to get yourself started on making an informed decision, you should pull together some important state specific resources to keep on hand that will make evaluating various concerns easier now and in the future. For instance, this is the time to gather information relevant to reporting in your state so that when you come upon a situation when you need to evaluate your concerns, you will have all the relevant information available to you to make the decision-making process smoother. Use the worksheets provided in this chapter to guide you on what information you need and to help you keep track of this information.

Question	Helpful Resource	Your Answer
What state are you in?	If you don't know, ask someone nearby… ;)	
What is the phone number professional reporters call to make a report to CPS in your state?	If you don't know, conduct a quick internet search for "child abuse reporting in [insert your state here]."	
Is the state you are in a Universal Reporting State?	Refer to this list from 2022: DE, FL, ID, IN, KY, MD, MS, NE, NH, NJ, NM, NC, OK, RI, TN, TX, UT, WY	
What is the legal threshold for suspicion in your state that requires a mandated reporter to call CPS?	If you don't know, call the CPS hotline for guidance or refer to this resource: https://www.childwelfare.gov/pubpdfs/manda.pdf	

Does your state (or locality) have a specific age at which children can be left home alone?	As of 2022, there were only 3 such states: IL (14 years old); MD (8 years old); and OR (10 years old). Some other states have "guidance" language.

Outlining the Decision-Making Framework

When professionals are faced with concerns that they think might require a report to CPS, they are often concerned they aren't doing the right thing or are confused. This reaction is perfectly normal. The following decision-making framework is designed to give professional reporters guidance through this confusing and concerning process.

The first step in the decision-making framework is **"Evaluating Your Concerns."** This process will involve asking questions about your concerns to see if they relate to child maltreatment, or not. If you determine that your concerns relate to child maltreatment, then you move on to the second step which is **"Determining If a Report is Required."**

Many reporters assume that if they have concerns, then they must make a report to CPS. However, not all concerns are required to be reported to CPS. The framework will help you determine the differences.

Evaluating Your Concerns

There are five main questions to answer before even considering if you are required to make a report to CPS:

1. What type(s) of maltreatment are you concerned might be happening?
2. What physical indicators are present, if any?
3. What behavioral indicators are present, if any?

4. Who might be responsible for the concerns you have? Is the alleged perpetrator of that maltreatment covered by the definition of child maltreatment in your state?
5. Do YOUR concerns meet the definition(s) of maltreatment?

Question	Helpful Resources	Answer
What type(s) of maltreatment are you concerned might be occurring?	Chapter 4	____ Neglect ____ Physical Abuse ____ Sexual Abuse ____ Em Ab/ Psy Mal
What physical indicators are present, if any?	Chapter 4	
What behavioral indicators are present, if any?	Chapter 4	
Who might be responsible for the concerns you have? And, is the alleged perpetrator appropriate to a report to CPS in your state?	You can call the CPS hotline for guidance, or refer to this resource: https://www.childwelfare.gov/pubpdfs/manda.pdf.	

Do YOUR concerns meet the definition(s) of maltreatment?	Consider your concerns in light of the definitions, indicators, and perpetrator questions you've answered.	____ **Yes** (Continue to **Evaluating Your Concerns.**) ____ **No** (See Ch. 6) ____ **Not Sure** (Continue to the next section.)

What type(s) of maltreatment are you concerned might be happening?

This seems like an easy one, but in practice it isn't so easy. Consider your concerns. Now, identify which of the types of maltreatment outlined in Chapter 4 your concerns relate to. You can have concerns for multiple types of maltreatment, or just one. However, if your concerns don't relate to any of these types of maltreatment, you are probably not required to make a report to CPS.

Here are your options:

- **Neglect** (Including Physical Neglect, Educational Neglect, Medical Neglect, Inadequate Supervision, and, in some states, Excessive Corporal Punishment)
- **Physical Abuse**
- **Sexual Abuse**
- **Emotional Abuse/Psychological Maltreatment**

What indicators are present?

Once you identify the type, or multiple types, of maltreatment that you suspect might be occurring, you need to consider what **physical**

and behavioral indicators are present that suggest that your concerns relate to the type(s) of maltreatment you have identified. In other words, what have you seen or heard that makes you think that maltreatment might be occurring? You can look back at Chapter 4 for guidance on what indicators are often associated with different types of maltreatment. However, remember that the list of indicators is not exhaustive and that not all indicators mean maltreatment is occurring.

If there are no physical or behavioral indicators present, are you concerned about the future probability of harm to a child caused by conditions they are being subjected to now? If so, please make note about these concerns for consideration later in your analysis.

Who might be responsible for the concerns you have?

Next, you should consider who might be responsible for the concerns you have. Not all alleged perpetrators of child maltreatment can be reported to CPS. Some alleged perpetrators can only be reported to law enforcement. Parents, whether they have legal custody of the child or not, can always be the subject of a report to CPS. Additionally, all adults living in the house with a child, or often found in the child's house, can also be reported.

In some states, perpetrators of child physical abuse or sexual abuse who do not reside with the child cannot be reported to CPS. In those states, reports can be made to the police, but are generally not required by law. In some states, certain mandated reporters (usually school employees) must make reports of sexual abuse if the perpetrator works in a school. If you have concerns that relate to a perpetrator who is not a parent and is not an adult who lives in the house with the child, you can call the CPS hotline for guidance.

If you are not sure who is responsible for the maltreatment, you might still need to make the report. You are not required to identify the perpetrator when making a report to CPS.

Do YOUR concerns meet the definition(s) of maltreatment?

Now that you've thought about your concerns and reminded yourself about definitions and indicators, you should consider whether your concerns meet a definition of any type of maltreatment. If your concerns don't meet a definition of any type of maltreatment, you likely do not need to make a report to CPS.

It is completely possible that you have concerns, valid concerns, for a child based on what you have observed or been told, but that the concerns do not rise to the definition of maltreatment. In these cases, you should not make a report to CPS. However, there is still much you can do to help the child and the family. We will explore these options in Chapter 6.

If you have determined that your concerns DO meet a definition of maltreatment, you need to next consider whether you are required to report your concerns to CPS.

Determining If a Report is Required

If you have determined that your concerns DO meet a definition of maltreatment, you should next consider whether you are required to report your concerns to CPS. There are five key questions to guide this part of the decision-making process:

1. Are you required to make a report based on your role?
2. Are your concerns about maltreatment already occurring or may potentially occur in the future?
3. Are you being objective?
4. Do your concerns meet the level of suspicion of maltreatment that requires a report to CPS?
5. Are you required to make this report to CPS?

Are you required to make a report based on your role?

First, we need to know if you are bound by the rules of a universal reporting state. You should know whether or not you are in a universal reporting state by now.

If you are bound by the rules of a universal reporting state, you are required to report your concerns to CPS when they rise to the level of suspicion of maltreatment that requires a report in your state NO MATTER WHAT YOUR ROLE IS IN RELATION TO YOUR CONCERNS. This means that if you have developed these concerns based on information gained through your professional role, you would be required to make a report. If you developed these concerns based on information you gained through a personal role, like from family, friends, and/or neighbors, you would STILL be required to make a report.

If you are NOT bound by the rules of a universal reporting state, you are ONLY required to report your concerns to CPS when they rise to the level of suspicion of maltreatment that requires a report in your state, AND YOU DEVELOPED YOUR CONCERNS THROUGH YOUR PROFESSIONAL ROLE. This means that if you have developed these concerns based on information you gained through your professional role, you would be required to make a report. But, if you have not developed these concerns based on information you gained through your personal role, you would NOT be required to make a report.

There are some additional issues you might need to consider related to the source of the information which depend on which state you are in. In some states, only information gathered or observed firsthand triggers a requirement to report. In other words, in those states, if someone told you about conditions that they observed (but you didn't) that created your concerns, you might not be required to make a report. The reason for this limitation is that information you receive from other people might not be reliable. If you're not sure what the standard is in your state, you can look at your state statute here: https://www.child-welfare.gov/pubpdfs/manda.pdf, or call the CPS hotline in your state for guidance.

Are your concerns related to harm that has already occurred or is potentially occurring in the future?

If your concerns are based on harm to a child that has already occurred, you can move on to the next step to determine if a report to CPS is required.

If your concerns are based on the potential of harm to a child, you should consider the "imminence" of harm. If harm has not yet occurred to the child, but you are concerned that harm will occur to a child if there is no intervention, consider whether harm will DEFINITELY occur if you don't make a call to CPS. Are there interventions that could prevent harm from occurring without a call to CPS? If there are things that you could do to help a family avoid harming a child, then by all means, please do so. For instance, if there is a chance the parent could address your concerns, thus mitigating the risk of harm, then talk to the parent about your concerns and help them address them by providing resources or recommendations. In cases where there is no harm to a child, as of yet, and the risk of harm is not imminent, a report to CPS is likely not required.

Are you being objective?

First of all, thank you for considering this question. Sometimes we make judgements about other people based on feelings and experiences that we might not even be aware are influencing us. When determining whether we need to make a report to CPS, we DO NOT want our personal feelings and experiences clouding our professional judgement. To avoid doing this, we need to explore the lens through which we are viewing the situation and check our privileges and biases.

Ask yourself, "Are you suspicious about parental behavior because they're not doing what you would do as a parent?" If so, think about whether the parents here are actually doing something wrong, or just doing something you are uncomfortable with.

Throughout the process of developing suspicions and then making a determination to make a report or not, you will have an experience unique to you, and unlike no other. This is because we each have our own experiences.

When I make a report to CPS, it is as a lawyer and a social worker with two decades of expertise in the area. I am also experiencing my role as a middle-aged, highly educated, White mother of a teenage son who has lived a largely upper-middle class, urban lifestyle. All of these parts of my experience influence what indicators of abuse and maltreatment I see and how I see them. These are the personal lenses through which I see the world around me.

The clients that I usually come in contact with during my professional practice are very different from me. My economic privilege means that I have never wondered if I have enough money to feed my family or pay my rent. I do not know what choices I would make in a tough financial situation. I do not have a history of addiction, but I have experiences with loved ones who have grappled with addiction and the impact on their children and family. When I work with a family struggling with addiction, I need to be aware about how my own experiences with my family members might be impacting how I view the case in front of me, for better or for worse.

When I'm evaluating my suspicions, I stop and think about whether my concerns and suspicions are credible or if I'm judging people because they are different from me, or not meeting MY expectations of myself as a parent.

No one can expect a reporter to leave their experiences behind when they're working. It's just not realistic to do so. However, by considering the impact of your experiences on how you see and evaluate the world around you, you CAN be more mindful about whether what you see is what is objectively being experienced. The more we consider these conditions, the better for our practice as professionals and people.

Do your concerns meet the level of suspicion of maltreatment that requires a report to CPS?

Each state's mandated reporting law defines a level of suspicion at which point a mandated reporter is required by law to report their concerns to CPS. Some common levels of suspicion used in state laws that trigger the requirement to make a report to CPS include:

- "Reasonableness," including "reasonable cause" to suspect/know, "reasonable cause to believe"/ "reasonable belief"
- "Reason to know" or "reason to believe"
- "Cause to believe" or "cause to suspect"
- "Knowledge of maltreatment" or "knows"
- "Good faith" suspicion or knowledge
- "Learns or comes to suspect"

The legal standard most frequently used in state law relates to "reasonableness." While we will focus on the reasonableness standard, it would be appropriate to use the same framework for considering your suspicions, no matter what specific legal standard is defined in your state.

The standards that trigger a required report to CPS in all states are generally considered low standards. Reasonable cause to suspect child maltreatment, and all similar thresholds, does not mean that the reporter needs to be prepared to prove maltreatment is occurring. Far from it. A report to CPS is generally considered as a formal request for an investigation into the reporter's concerns. A determination of maltreatment from a resulting investigation generally requires a higher standard of proof than that required to mandate a report.

Even though the threshold to require a report is considered low, reporters' suspicions still are expected to be "reasonable." How do you know if you're being "reasonable?" "Reasonable" means having sound judgement, or being fair and sensible. In the context of legal considerations, a reasonable decision is one that is appropriate or legitimate, given the circumstances. It's possible that someone thinks they're being reasonable, even when they're not.

When considering reasonableness, a helpful question to frame the analysis is: "Would someone with similar knowledge and information feel the same way?" When you consider what other people might think, you remove the hazards to reasonableness, which can be subjective, like the lens of your personal and professional experiences through which you view the case.

The best way to check if you're being reasonable in your suspicions of child maltreatment is to confer with someone who has similar training and experience, but perhaps a different perspective. These people, generally colleagues and supervisors, can help you determine if you are over-reacting or if you have legitimate concerns.

If, after consulting with them, you no longer have suspicions of abuse or maltreatment, then you don't need to make a report (and you could look to Chapter 6 for further guidance).

If, after consulting with them, you still think a report is required, then you can do so confidently knowing that you explored your reasoning for making the call and are confident you are being reasonable. If you confer with colleagues or supervisors and they tell you NOT to make a report, please note, it is YOUR responsibility to make a report when you have the requisite level of suspicion. No one can tell you not to make a report.

Are You Required to Make THIS Report to CPS?

Anyone can make a report to CPS. You don't have to be a mandated reporter to make a report. But only mandated reporters are REQUIRED TO make reports.

If you determine that your level of suspicion does not meet the standard in your state that requires a report or your concerns don't meet a definition of maltreatment, then you do not need to make a report. Instead, think of how you could support the family and ultimately protect the child without CPS intervention. Are there programs or resources you could connect them to? How else could you help? We will explore these options in Chapter 6.

If you determine that your level of suspicion DOES meet the standard in your state that requires a report and that your concerns meet a definition of maltreatment relevant in your state, then the law requires you to make a report to CPS. We will explore this process in Chapter 7.

Question	Helpful Resources	Answer
Are you required to make a report based on your role?	In universal reporting states, reports required regardless of role. In other states, reports only required when concerns develop through professional role.	

Are your concerns related to harm that has already occurred or may potentially occur in the future?	If yes, continue to next question. If your concerns are related to potential harm in the future, you need to consider imminence.	
Are you being objective?	Think about how your personal lens through which you view this case might be impacting your judgement.	
Do your concerns meet the level of suspicion of maltreatment that requires a report to CPS?	The requisite level of suspicion in your state can be found here: https://www.childwelfare.gov/pubpdfs/manda.pdf.	
Are you required to make this report to CPS?	Consider your concerns in light of all the questions you have considered through this process.	____ **Yes** (See Ch. 7) ____ **No** (See Ch. 6) ____ **Not Sure**

Applying the Decision-Making Framework

Let's use some of the case examples we started to explore in Chapter 4 to practice applying the decision-making framework we learned in this chapter. We will make assumptions for some of the first questions in the framework, using three different state experiences, and start with the clearest case example provided:

A 5-year-old presents to their regular pediatrician's office with painful and reluctant urination. Urinalysis confirms a urinary tract infection. While waiting for the examination the child seems physically uncomfortable. A physical examination finds the child extremely protective of their body. When you inquire if they are ok, they say that someone hurt them "down there".

Question	Your Answer
What state are you in?	New York
What is the phone number professional reporters call to make a report to CPS in your state?	Mandated Reporters call: 1(800) 635-1522
Is the state you are in a Universal Reporting State?	NO
What is the legal threshold for suspicion in your state that requires a mandated reporter to call CPS?	Reasonable Cause to Suspect
Does your state (or locality) have a specific age at which children can be left home alone?	NO (but also, not relevant to this case)
What type(s) of maltreatment are you concerned might be occurring?	Sexual Abuse

What physical indicators are present, if any?	Physically uncomfortable Urinary tract infection
What behavioral indicators are present, if any?	Child's disclosure that someone hurt them "down there"
Who might be responsible for the concerns you have? And, is the alleged perpetrator appropriate to a report to CPS in your state?	UNCLEAR (Please note, if the alleged perpetrated is not a parent, or other legally responsible person, then a report to CPS might not be accepted in this case. The NYS CPS hotline would, instead, refer the case to law enforcement.)
Do YOUR concerns meet the definition(s) of maltreatment?	YES The child's behavioral and physical indicators suggest trauma to their genitalia which was possibly caused by a sexual act.
Are you required to make a report based on your role?	Yes. In NY, my direct contact professional contact with the child and the indicators I have observed would require a report based on my role.
Are your concerns related to harm that has already occurred or may potentially occur in the future?	My concerns are based on harm that has already occurred.

Are you being objective?	Good question. I conferred with my colleague, who has met the child and family. My colleague is similarly concerned based on the indicators present. I believe I am being objective.
Do your concerns meet the level of suspicion of maltreatment that requires a report to CPS?	While it is possible that the child's condition could have been created by conditions that are not abusive, it is more likely based on the child's disclosure that the cause was abuse. Therefore, I believe my suspicions are reasonable.
Are you required to make this report to CPS?	YES. I believe I have reasonable cause to suspect child sexual abuse, and therefore, the law in New York State requires me to make a report to CPS on this case.

Let's explore a different case:

A 9-year-old child has a cold with a fever. After a few days, they develop a sinus infection. The parents seek medical intervention. During intake, you are told that the child was sent to school while they had a fever in order to receive breakfast and lunch through the school meal program. You also find out that the child rarely is served dinner at night.

Question	**Your Answer**
What state are you in?	Idaho

What is the phone number professional reporters call to make a report to CPS in your state?	Everyone in Idaho can call: 1-855-552-KIDS (5437), or 211
Is the state you are in a Universal Reporting State?	YES
What is the legal threshold for suspicion in your state that requires a mandated reporter to call CPS?	A person has reason to believe that a child has been abused, abandoned, or neglected, or A person observes a child being subjected to conditions or circumstances that would reasonably result in abuse, abandonment, or neglect.
Does your state (or locality) have a specific age at which children can be left home alone?	NO
What type(s) of maltreatment are you concerned might be occurring?	Neglect
What physical indicators are present, if any?	Sick child sent to school Food scarcity at home
What behavioral indicators are present, if any?	Child is hungry

Who might be responsible for the concerns you have? And, is the alleged perpetrator appropriate to a report to CPS in your state?	Parents. Yes. Parents can be reported to CPS.
Do YOUR concerns meet the definition(s) of maltreatment?	Unclear.
Are you required to make a report based on your role?	In Idaho, all adults are mandated reporters. So, I would be required to make a report if my suspicions met the reasonable belief threshold, regardless of my role with the child and family.
Are your concerns related to harm that has already occurred or may potentially occur in the future?	My concerns are not based on harm that has already occurred. I am concerned about potential harm to the child.
Are you being objective?	Good question. I conferred with my colleague, who has met the child and family. We are both concerned about the child being sent to school sick, but we agree that the parents weren't trying to hurt the child, but were trying to help the child.
Do your concerns meet the level of suspicion of maltreatment that requires a report to CPS?	I do not reasonably believe the child has been neglected, nor are they in imminent danger of being neglected.

| Are you required to make this report to CPS? | No. I do not believe that I am required to make a report to CPS. I am going to work with the family so that they don't have to make this difficult choice again. |

Let's try one more. You find out that a 10-year-old was left home alone for 9 hours on a weekend while their parent is at work.

Question	Your Answer
What state are you in?	Oregon
What is the phone number professional reporters call to make a report to CPS in your state?	Mandated Reporters call: 1-855-503-SAFE (7233)
Is the state you are in a Universal Reporting State?	NO
What is the legal threshold for suspicion in your state that requires a mandated reporter to call CPS?	Reasonable cause to believe
Does your state (or locality) have a specific age at which children can be left home alone?	Yes. 10 years old, but the state provides guidance here: https://www.oregon.gov/DHS/CHILDREN/CHILD-ABUSE/Documents/ORCAH-FAQs.pdf
What type(s) of maltreatment are you concerned might be occurring?	Neglect

What physical indicators are present, if any?	None
What behavioral indicators are present, if any?	Child was left alone for 9 hours
Who might be responsible for the concerns you have? And, is the alleged perpetrator appropriate to a report to CPS in your state?	Parents. Yes. Parents can be reported to CPS.
Do YOUR concerns meet the definition(s) of maltreatment?	The law in Oregon says children under the age of 10 years old shouldn't be left alone (with exceptions). This child is 10 years old, and thus can be left alone. However, if the child was endangered through this action, regardless of age, it could be neglect.
Are you required to make a report based on your role?	If I developed this information based on my professional role, then in Oregon I'm a mandated reporter. If I developed this information based on personal (non-professional) relationships to the child and/or family, then in Oregon I'm not a mandated reporter.
Are your concerns related to harm that has already occurred or may potentially occur in the future?	My concerns are not based on harm that has already occurred. I am concerned about potential harm to the child.

	Good question. I conferred with a colleague, who has knows the child and family. We are both concerned about the child being left alone for so long, but we agree that their parents weren't trying to endanger the child.
Are you being objective?	
Do your concerns meet the level of suspicion of maltreatment that requires a report to CPS?	I do not reasonably believe the child has been neglected, nor are they in imminent danger of being neglected.
Are you required to make this report to CPS?	No. I do not believe that I am required to make a report to CPS. I am going to work with the family to make sure the child is safe if they have to be left alone for that long.

Test Questions

You find out that a 10-year-old child you see in your practice stole some small articles from the local drug store. Their mother spanked them, causing bruises and welts. The bruises and welts are considered:

   a. Behavioral indicators of maltreatment
   b. Physical indicators of maltreatment
   c. Universal Reporters
   d. Imminent Harm

The most common state-level legal standard for requiring suspicions to be reported to CPS is related to the concept of:

a. Confidence
b. Knowledge
c. Professionalism
d. Reasonableness

To avoid the influence of bias in our reporting to CPS, we should:

a. Think about whether the parents in the case are actually doing something wrong, or just doing something we are uncomfortable with.
b. Explore the lens through which we are viewing the situation.
c. Check our privileges and biases.
d. All of the answers are appropriate to employ in order to avoid the influence of bias in our report to CPS.

The legal thresholds that suspicions of child maltreatment must meet in order to be required by law in a given state:

a. Are generally considered low thresholds
b. Are generally considered high thresholds
c. Require the mandated reporter to be 100% maltreatment is occurring
d. Require the mandated reporter to be "confident" that maltreatment is occurring

If you determine that your suspicions meet the definition of at least one type of maltreatment, next, you should:

a. Make a report to CPS
b. Call the police
c. Evaluate whether your suspicions are required to be reported to CPS
d. Work with the family to mitigate the risk of harm

Discussion Questions

- Were your evaluations of the example cases similar to mine? If not, how did they differ? And, what do you think the differences show?
- How would you define the "lens" through which you see the world? How might your experiences as a child, and not adult, differ from that of your patients? How might they be similar? How might these differences (or similarities) impact how you view the cases where you have concerns about child maltreatment?

Important Resources & References

Child Welfare Information Gateway (2019). Mandatory Reporters of Child Abuse and Neglect, https://www.childwelfare.gov/pubpdfs/manda.pdf

This resource is EXTREMELY helpful when trying to determine if you are a mandated reporter in a given state, whether a state is a universal reporting state, and when you need to determine the threshold of suspicion needed to require a report. HINT: Use the text search function to find your state.

Making the Tough Call (2021). Decision-Making Framework Worksheet.
On the next page, you can find a blank form to use when trying to make the decision whether you are required to make a report to CPS based on your concerns for child maltreatment.

WORKSHEET

Question	Helpful Resource	Your Answer
What state are you in?	If you don't know, ask someone nearby... ;)	
What is the phone number professional reporters call to make a report to CPS in your state?	Conduct a quick internet search for "child abuse reporting in [insert your state here]"	
Is the state you are in an Universal Reporting State?	Refer to this list from 2022: DE, FL, ID, IN, KY, MD, MS, NE, NH, NJ, NM, NC, OK, RI, TN, TX, UT, WY	
What is the legal threshold for suspicion in your state that requires a mandated reporter to call CPS?	Call the CPS hotline in your state for guidance, or refer to this resource: https://www.childwelfare.gov/pubpdfs/manda.pdf	

WORKSHEET

Question	Helpful Resource	Your Answer
Does your state (or locality) have a specific age at which children can be left home alone?	As of 2022, there were only 3 such states: IL (14 years old); MD (8 years old); and OR (10 years old). Some other states have "guidance" language.	
What type(s) of maltreatment are you concerned might be occurring?	Chapter 4	___ Neglect ___ Physical Abuse ___ Sexual Abuse ___ Em Ab/ Psy Mal
What physical indicators are present, if any?	Chapter 4	
What behavioral indicators are present, if any?	Chapter 4	

WORKSHEET

Question	Helpful Resource	Your Answer
Who might be responsible for the concerns you have? And, is the alleged perpetrator appropriate to a report to CPS in your state?	Call the CPS hotline in your state for guidance, or refer to this resource: https://www.childwelfare.gov/pubpdfs/manda.pdf	
Do YOUR concerns meet the definition(s) of maltreatment?	Consider your concerns in light of the definitions, indicators and perpetrator questions you've answered.	___ Yes (Continue evaluating your concerns) ___ No (See Ch. 6) ___ Not Sure (Continue evaluating your concerns)
Are you required to make a report based on your role?	In universal reporting states, reports required regardless of role. In other states, reports only required when concerns develop through professional role.	

WORKSHEET

Question	Helpful Resource	Your Answer
Are your concerns related to harm that has already occurred, or potentially occurring in the future?	If yes, continue next question. If your concerns are related to potential harm in the future, you need to consider imminence.	
Are you being objective?	This is the time to think about how your personal lens through which you view this case might be impacting your judgment.	
Do your concerns meet the level of suspicion of maltreatment that requires a report to CPS?	The requisite level of suspicion in your state can be found here: https://www.childwelfare.gov/pubpdfs/ manda.pdf.	

WORKSHEET

Question	Helpful Resource	Your Answer
Are you required to make this report to CPS?	Consider your concerns in light of all the questions you have considered through this process.	____ Yes (See Ch. 7) ____ No (See Ch. 6) ____ Not Sure (Further guidance can be found in Chapters 6 &7)

6

When You Decide NOT to Make
a Report

Guidance for professional reporters of child maltreatment usually centers around what to do after deciding to make a report to CPS. We will present that process, and relevant considerations, in Chapter 7. Based on research, professional reporters who have concerns are more likely to decide not to make a report than to make a report. So, this chapter presents guidance on what professional reporters should do when they make the more common decision NOT to make a report to CPS.

Clarifying the Decision to NOT Make a Report

When a professional reporter decides NOT make a report to CPS, the decision could be based on one or more of various reasons. In general, the multitude of possible reasons fall into two broad categories:

- Reporter does not believe that their concerns rise to a level of suspicion of child maltreatment that requires a report to CPS, or
- Reporter believes that their concerns DO rise to a level of suspicion of child maltreatment that requires a report to CPS, but the reporter chooses not to report to CPS.

When a professional reporter mandated to make a report by the law in the relevant state chooses not to make a report because they believe their concerns do not rise to a level of suspicion that requires a report to CPS, they should be protected from liability for "failure to report." There is not a "failure to report" in this situation because the professional made the reasoned decision that a report was not required.

Liability for "failing to make a report" to CPS generally depends on the mandated reporter "knowingly" or "willfully" choosing not to make a report to CPS when the law requires them to do so. The terms "knowingly" or "willfully" relate to legal standards of culpability or responsibility. "Knowingly" failing to make a report to CPS involves a reporter having knowledge or awareness that they are required to make a report of certain suspicions and not making the report, not because of a mistake, accident or some other innocent reason. "Willfully" failing to make a report, similarly, means that the reporter deliberately did not make a report to CPS when they had the knowledge that they were required by law to make a report. Neither "knowingly" or "willfully" requires the reporter to have ill or evil intentions. The use of a decision-making framework, like that outlined in Chapter 5, by a professional reporter that resulted in the decision that a report was not required should insulate the reporter from liability for "failure to report." The evaluation provided by the use of the framework would be evidence that the reporter neither "knowingly" nor "willfully" avoided their legal obligation to report.

However, when a professional reporter mandated to make a report by the law in the relevant state chooses not to make a report when they believe they are mandated to do so, they are subject to liability for failing to make a report.

In either case, the professional should consider how to document and communicate their concerns as well as consider how they, in their professional role, can support the child and family that they are concerned about.

Documenting the Decision to NOT Make a Report

When a professional reporter mandated to make a report by the law in the relevant state chooses not to make a report to CPS because their concerns did not rise to a level of suspicion that requires a report to CPS, they should document their decision and the process used to arrive at that decision in "contemporaneous" written notes.

Contemporaneous written notes are notes the reporter makes at the time they make the decision not to report, or shortly thereafter. These notes can be made by hand or written into a computerized/electronic document. Regardless of the form, the notes should be dated. The reporter should make sure they have access to these records for at least 2-10 years. The length of time the records should be retained relates to the statute of limitations for criminal and civil liability and varies by state. Contemporaneous written notes can help shield the reporter from legal liability in the future if they are ever accused of failing to make a report.

Contemporaneous notes, as opposed to verbal recollection or notes long after the occurrence, are considered the most valid source of reliable recollection. These notes should outline the reporter's concerns and clearly highlight how the reporter contemplated the legal requirement to report but decided their concerns did not rise to a level of suspicion that they believe required a report. Such notes could discuss how the concerns did not match with legal definitions of types of maltreatment, etc.

Reporters who believed they were required to make a report, but chose not to, should understand that whatever they document in their notes may be discoverable and admissible during a civil or criminal proceeding against them for failure to report.

Communicating Concerns

When a reporter makes the decision not to make a report to CPS, the reporter may still choose to communicate their concerns with colleagues and supervisors and/or the family of concern. It is important to note that there is no obligation to discuss your concerns with anyone unless your employer has a protocol or policy related to this type of situation.

Whether required or not, it can be very helpful to communicate with colleagues and/or supervisors about concerns you might have about patients. As previously discussed, it can be helpful to consult with colleagues and/or supervisors while undergoing the decision-making process. It can also be helpful to consult with colleagues and/or supervisors after making the decision to not make a report to CPS. At this point, you can seek recommendations for continued work with the patient, find relevant articles that might be helpful to your continued work on the case, or with similar cases in the future, and/or gather referral resources to offer the patient. It is important to ensure that the confidentiality protections afforded to your relationship with your patient are preserved in the communications with your colleagues and/ or supervisors. If you work for the same agency, then such protections are assumed for all who are employed by the agency. If you consult with a supervisor or colleagues outside your organization, it is important to contract with them to ensure a continuation of the confidentiality protections or avoid any sharing of identifiable information about your patient.

Even though you have made a decision to not make a report to CPS, you should consider communicating your concerns to your patient, or their family, whenever appropriate. This communication can simply be intended to inform the family about your concerns, educate them about definitions of child maltreatment, and help them understand their rights, and the limitations thereof, or aimed to encourage a change in behavior that would negate a future risk of harm to the child.

Addressing Risk through Professional Practice

You've recognized an area of concern for a family you are working with. You don't think your concerns rise to a level of suspicion that requires a report to CPS, but you're worried. You might be concerned about a future risk of maltreatment or simply think the family needs help. While many professional reporters choose to make a report to CPS and hope that CPS intervention can provide the family with the help they need, you have another option. You, as a medical and/or healthcare professional, might be able to mitigate the risk of maltreatment through your professional practice with the child and/or family.

As a medical and/or healthcare professional, you are empowered through your role to support healthy family function and protect children by:

- Identifying appropriate services or resources that the family needs to address a presenting problem,
- Making a referral for treatment for mental health concerns or substance use disorders,
- Providing a sounding board for the parents to inform their problem solving,
- Listening to the frustrations of a parent who doesn't know what to do to make a situation better, and/or
- Many other options, depending on the specific presenting circumstance.

There are MANY things professional reporters can do, and in some cases doing one or more of these things will actually reduce the risk of harm and, thus, could prevent us from developing the requisite level of suspicion that would require a call to CPS under mandated reporting laws.

Isn't the ultimate goal to protect children and support families? Supporting healthy families prevents maltreatment and is the ultimate way of protecting children. As medical and healthcare professionals, of all people, you are in a great position to do just that.

Test Questions

True/False: You can only be held responsible for failing to report a case to CPS if you had evil or ill intentions.

You have determined that a family you are working with is at high risk of neglecting their child. What is your best option for responding to your concerns?

a. Immediately make a report to CPS.
b. Assist the family to identify resources that can help mitigate the risk.
c. Tell the family about your concerns and that they need to show you progress soon, or you're going to report them.
d. Tell your supervisor so that they can talk to the family.

A child is diagnosed with leukemia. Their treatment team recommends bone marrow transplant (aka stem cell transfer). The family are members of a "faith-healing" religious group, who believe that God will cure the child as long as the family prays appropriately and lives piously. Which of the following choices best defines the appropriate response for the professional reporters who interact with the family?

a. Make an immediate report of medical neglect to child protective services.
b. Tell the parents that if they don't consent to treatment, their child will be taken away.
c. Explain to the parents that the treatment is necessary to save the child's life and, therefore, the reporter will seek government assistance to secure such treatment, if necessary.

    d. Pray for the child and respect the parents' religious beliefs.

    e. Call the police.

A public school district has adopted a new sex education program that aims to inform children 10 years and older about contraception. A family you work with has strict religious beliefs against contraception. The parents decide to home-school their children instead of subjecting their children to such an environment. Which of the following choices best describes an appropriate response for professional reporters who interact with the family?

    a. Make an immediate report of educational neglect to child protective services.

    b. Tell the parents that if they don't enroll their children in a public or approved private school, their children will be taken away.

    c. Explain to the parents that contraception education does not correlate with higher rates of sex amongst teenagers.

    d. Explain to the parents that they have the right to home-school their children, but they need to follow the applicable law in their state in order to meet compulsory education requirements for their children.

    e. Call the police.

A family you are working with has one 5-year-old child. They take good care of the child, but after significant experiences with illness and death in the family, the parents are extremely worried the child will contract a disease. As a result, they don't allow the child to attend school or socialize with other children. What would be the most appropriate professional response to this case?

    a. Leave the situation to the family.

b. Help the family seek a community agency or other resources to address their anxiety and safely ensure the child's education and socialization.

c. Make a report to CPS.

d. Call the police Immediately.

Discussion Questions

- Consider your current case file documentation policy and practice. Do you feel like your current documentation policy and practice adequately protects you from liability if you were to decide not to make a report to CPS? Why? Why not?
- What considerations should you make when communicating with a patient or family about your concerns, even though you decided not to make a report to CPS? Role-play this conversation.

Resources

Child Welfare Information Gateway, United States Department of Health & Human Services, Administration on Children and Families (2019). Penalties for failure to report and false reporting of child abuse and neglect https://www.childwelfare.gov/pubpdfs/report.pdf

United States Department of Justice (2020). Criminal resource manual, 910. Knowingly and willfully. https://www.justice.gov/archives/jm/criminal-resource-manual-910-knowingly-and-willfully

7

When You Decide to MAKE a Report

Clarifying Your Decision to Make a Report to CPS

When a professional reporter decides to make a report to CPS, the decision could be based on one or more of various reasons. In general, the multitude of possible reasons fall into two broad categories:

- Reporter's concern rises to a level of suspicion of child maltreatment that requires a report to CPS, or
- Reporter's concern does not rise to a level of suspicion of child maltreatment that would require a report to CPS, but the reporter seeks intervention from CPS in this particular situation, usually with the goal of protecting the child from future harm or helping the family.

When the professional reporter believes that their concern rises to a level of suspicion that requires a report to CPS, then making a report to CPS will fulfill their legal obligation as a mandated reporter and insulate them from liability for failure to report. When the professional reporter's concerns do not rise to a level of suspicion of child maltreatment that would require a report to CPS, the reporter would not be subject to failure to report liability if they did not make the report to CPS.

Any reporter making the decision to call CPS under either of these two broad categories is protected from legal action if the resulting investigation does not find significant evidence of child maltreatment; both categories involve reports that are made in good faith out of concern for the child and/or family. This legal protection is called "immunity." Any reporter, however, that makes a report without good faith concern for the child or family (or in "bad faith") will not be protected by immunity provisions. "Bad faith" reports involve making a report to CPS about circumstances that the reporter knows are untrue or exaggerated. Reports made in bad faith are considered "false reports" and punishable under civil and criminal law in all states.

Preparing to Make a Report to CPS

When a mandated reporter makes the decision to report to CPS, they are generally required by law to "immediately" file that report. However, the reporter does not need to automatically pick up the phone; they can do what they need to in order to adequately prepare for making the call. It is helpful, for instance, to gather all relevant documents and notes or open related files on an accessible computer. Relevant documents may contain names and contact information for the child and family members, including dates of birth, when known. Documents that relate to relevant information about the alleged perpetrator, including name and contact information, are also helpful.

In many states, mandated reporters are required to follow up their call to CPS by submitting a specific form completed with related information. If you can obtain a copy of that form, it is recommended practice to complete a draft version of the form before you make the call to CPS. Usually, the questions the CPS hotline worker will ask relate to the items on that form. If you complete the form to the best of your ability before the call, you will be well prepared for the interaction with the hotline worker. If you don't have the answers to all the items on the form, do not worry; complete what you can and leave blank what you don't know.

Find a comfortable place to sit in a private location. Phone calls to CPS hotlines are not short; they take, on average, 15 minutes. The reporter should be prepared to dedicate their full attention to the call and should avoid distractions, wherever possible. If you are nervous about making the call, you could practice through role-play exercises with a colleague or supervisor or practice on your own, prior to making the call.

Actually Making a Report to CPS

Making a report to CPS involves making a phone call. To find the phone number to call in your state, you can use the link, here:

https://www.childwelfare.gov/organizations/?CWIGFunctionsaction=rols:main.dspList&rolType=Custom&RS_ID=5

You can also find the phone number by conducting a simple internet search with terms like "reporting suspected child abuse in [your state]." In many states, there are separate phone numbers to call if you are a mandated reporter, as opposed to a non-mandated reporter. In cases where there are not enough hotline workers for the volume of calls received at a given time, priority is given to calls coming in over the mandated reporter hotline number.

When your call is answered by a CPS hotline worker, they will ask for your name, contact information, and concerns. Mandated reporters in all states will need to provide their identity and should not remain anonymous. Professional reporters should make clear their relationship to the patient and their professional role.

The hotline worker will ask for information about the family you have concerns about, including names, approximate ages, demographics, and contact information. They will also ask the reporter to explain their suspicions and concerns.

The hotline worker is interested in details as well as impressions. It won't be enough to say that you think the child is a victim of abuse or neglect. You will need to explain what behavioral and/or physical indicators you have witnessed and when. You will be asked to identify which type(s) of maltreatment you suspect the child has been subjected to.

The hotline worker will ask for information about the alleged perpetrator. They will ask for names, contact information, and other identifying information. They might ask you if the alleged perpetrator has any prior history of perpetration of abuse or neglect.

The hotline worker will ask a lot of questions. These questions might include whether you know where the child is currently, if the child has siblings, if the child has special needs, or whether the child is on medication. They might want to know if the family speaks a language other than English so that they can ensure someone who speaks that language is involved in the investigation. The hotline worker should ask if there are personal safety issues you are aware of, like weapons in the home or a history of violent behavior. They will ask you if there is any other information that you could provide that would be helpful to investigators, including whether you believe the child is in imminent danger.

If you don't know the answer to any particular question, just say you don't know. It's okay.

For a video example of a call to CPS, check out this video:

https://www.youtube.com/watch?v=gIVzg3ZDwuI
(Please note, the video is from New York State, and references the "SCR." The "SCR" in New York State is the "State Central Register of Child Abuse and Maltreatment" and is the entity that accepts CPS reports by telephone hotline.)

Document the context of your reporting experience through your case notes. Make sure to note the date and time of your call, the number you called, and any identifier provided by the CPS worker (like their name or worker identification number).

What If CPS Won't Take Your Report?

In cases where CPS does not accept your report for investigation, they should provide you with a reason. If you do not understand the reason they provide, you should ask for clarification. If you still don't understand, you should ask to speak to a supervisor. Do not worry about offending the hotline worker. If you are confused, they might be too. The supervisor will have more experience and a fresh perspective. The supervisor might be able to ask you questions that clarify the reasons your report was not accepted. You should document this important conversation through contemporaneous case notes. If your report is not accepted by CPS, they will likely not keep a significant record of your call. If, later, you are accused of failing to report, your case notes will insulate you from liability as evidence that you attempted to discharge your duty to report.

If the Family is Already in the Child Welfare System, Do You Still Report to CPS?

What about situations where you have a concern about a child already involved in the child protection system? Do you need to make another report?

A reporter does not need to make a new report of circumstances that they know are already being investigated. If you believe that the concerns you have identified are not already known to CPS, you can make a new report to the CPS hotline, but let them know the family is already involved in the system. Alternatively, you can contact the current CPS caseworker and tell them about these new concerns.

Reporters who want to confirm that they discharged their duty as a mandated reporter in those situations should contact the assigned CPS worker or CPS hotline for clarification. Take contemporaneous case notes regarding any conversations with the CPS caseworker.

What to Do in Cases Involving an Emergency

When you are confronted with a situation where you believe that immediate harm will occur to a child without intervening action, what should you do? You can call the CPS hotline and start the call by saying, "I have an emergency." The CPS hotline worker will help determine if you need to call 911 to get an appropriate level of intervention. Please note, the CPS hotline, itself, does not have the capacity to provide an immediate response. If you believe that the CPS hotline process would take too long to get an adequate response that would protect the child from impending harm, you should call 911 and explain your concerns.

Please note that most professional reporters are not authorized to keep children from their parents. However, CPS workers and police officers (as well as some hospital officials) have this authority.

Reporting in an Organizational Setting

While it is important to follow protocol for reporting outlined by your place of employment, it is also important to know your rights and obligations. You should notify your supervisor of your concerns of child maltreatment prior to making a report. Reporters should not have to get "approval" from supervisors in order to make a report, but it is usually helpful to process your concerns before making a call. Talking to a supervisor might help you determine that a report is not required or clarify that making a report is the appropriate decision. If your supervisor tells you not to make to a report to CPS, but you do so anyway because you believe it is your legal obligation to do so, the law in most states specifically protects you from retaliation by your employer for making a call in good faith.

It is the reporter's individually held responsibility to make a report once meeting the required threshold of suspicion that requires a report in your state. In fact, each mandated reporter who has the same knowledge and experience with the family is obligated to make the report.

If there are multiple reporters in one school, office, or agency with the same concern, each reporter does not need to make an individual report. The group of reporters can usually make one report together and have each of their names attached to the case. In such a situation, the reporter with the most direct knowledge should make the primary report and give the CPS hotline worker the names and contact information of the other mandated reporters. In some larger agencies and schools there is an administrator who makes the calls to CPS and keeps track of cases reported to CPS. This agency administrator is usually also responsible for coordinating follow-up communication with CPS through the investigation.

What does CPS do after you make a report?

After a report is made, CPS starts an investigation. The investigation usually starts within one day's time, and it can last up to two months. The length of time before an investigation must conclude is determined by state law and differs across the country.

CPS investigations involve collection of information from various sources, including:

- Contact with the reporting source
- Contact with the child(ren) on the report, including interviews and observations
- Contact with the parents of the child(ren) on the report, including interviews and observations
- Contact with other people named in the report, like non-parental perpetrators

- Contact with collateral sources, including schools, medical providers, and neighbors
- A home visit/inspection
- Documentary evidence from the report source and other sources.

At the end of the investigation, CPS makes a decision whether enough evidence exists to determine that maltreatment has occurred. If they find sufficient evidence of maltreatment, then CPS makes a decision about what interventions, if any, they will require of the family. These interventions can include removal of the child into what is called substitute care, including kinship or foster care placement. Other interventions can include mandating treatment or training programs or simply supervising the family over a period of time. There are a series of laws that direct the regularity through which CPS must review a family's case or close the case and end supervision.

It is important to note that in all states cases where investigations find adequate evidence of maltreatment will remain on the record of the responsible parties, usually a parent or parents, for a number of years. This length of time is dictated by state law. For instance, in New York State, a substantiated report will remain on the Child Abuse Registry Index ("CARI system") until 10 years after the youngest child on the report turns 18. So, if there is a newborn on a substantiated case in New York, the responsible parent might have a child abuse record for 28 years.

When someone has a record of child maltreatment, they might be unable to get a job in certain sectors, including childcare and education. These policies were originally made in an effort to protect children from predatory behavior when concern for child maltreatment was focused on physical and sexual abuse. Now, the vast majority of reports involve neglect. As a result, there are millions of parents who cannot access employment because of past behavior for which they have had no recurrence and which occurred decades before. There are, however, processes through which someone can challenge the existence of their

CARI record. Finding an attorney or other advocate to assist with this process is recommended.

Differential/Alternative Response

The term "differential response" defines a set of alternative approaches for a CPS initial intervention with families after a report is made to the hotline. Differential response is also called "alternative response," family assessment response, multiple response, or dual track. All these terms refer to a way of structuring CPS to allow for more flexibility in how to respond to low- and moderate-risk cases and better meet the needs of families. Differential response, however, is not yet available in all parts of the country.

Instead of focusing CPS efforts on investigation and intervention into a family, differential CPS response aims to provide protection for children by engaging families in a process to mutually identify and respond to family needs. There is growing awareness that traditional CPS responses to family concerns do not serve children and families well, especially since there are concerns for social and racial justice in the system. Differential response systems were designed to provide an alternative to the traditional investigation and intervention. The differential response practice links families with services that will strengthen their ability to safely care for their children, ultimately reducing the number of children entering foster care and decreasing future family involvement with the child welfare system.

The decision whether a report is met with a traditional investigation or through a differential response system is based on the concerns raised in the report. The hotline worker or the investigating caseworker are often responsible for making the determination whether the family should be offered the differential response track.

Concerns for Reporter Confidentiality

Many reporters are concerned a family will know that they made a report.

While all mandated reporters must provide their name and contact information when making a report to child protective services, it is against the law for CPS workers conducting an initial investigation to tell the family who made the report. However, if the report results in a court case, the reporter's identifying information will be included in the court file since the reporter is potentially a witness in a trial.

The reporter can give CPS permission to inform the family about their identity. Also, there is no law restricting the reporter from telling the family about the report themselves. In fact, many medical and healthcare professionals inform their patients about reports to CPS before they are made.

In some cases of sexual abuse and extreme physical abuse concerns, the reporter should not tell the family about the report, at least until after the investigation has started. The concern in these cases is that the child may be influenced by questions from family members, coached to deny the allegations, or otherwise be threatened or harmed.

Consider This Case

I made a report about a family that I work with. I didn't tell the parents about the report, but they confronted me and told me they know I made the report! How did this happen?

In my many years of practice in this area, I have worked with families who were subjects of reports. They usually knew exactly who made the report, even if no one from CPS or the reporter told them.

Think of it this way: in cases where the alleged maltreatment was not at all true, there usually aren't many people in a family's life who would make a false report, so the family knows quickly who made a harassing report against them. In cases where the alleged maltreatment is true or the concerns are based in fact, again, parents have a pretty good idea about who knows their business and, thus, generally know who made the call.

To avoid the potential for uncomfortable situations like these, the professional reporter should carefully consider their policy and practice around informed consent and informing patients when they make a report to CPS.

Choosing Whether to Inform Your Patient About a Report

Sometimes the hardest decision to make about reporting is whether to tell the patient that you're making the report. This is particularly difficult for medical and healthcare professionals who have ongoing relationships with patients. Many other professional reporters don't have an ongoing relationship with the family they report to CPS. And, even for some that do have an ongoing relationship with the patient after the call, the dynamics of their relationship are not necessarily integral to the work they do together.

Should you tell the patient you made the report or not? That decision is up to you. The law does NOT require you to inform your patient when you a make a report about them or their family.

When making the decision whether or not to tell your patient that you made a report to CPS, you can consider any concerns you have regarding your safety and that of your patient and other people. If you feel that anyone's safety would be in question were you to share this information with your patient, then, by all means, do not tell the patient that you made a report.

If you determine that no one's safety is at risk, then you can tell your patient, but you are still not required to. You should consider the impact that such a disclosure would have on your relationship with your patient and your patient's participation in whatever service they are receiving from you.

A patient may decide that they no longer want to receive services from the person who made a report to CPS. While this decision may be unfortunate, you also need to remember that the patient has the right to self-determination. In the case where a patient refuses to continue services with a professional because they made a report to CPS, the professional reporter should provide the patient the opportunity to work with another provider within their organization/network or provide a referral to a similar professional in another setting.

If you decide NOT to inform your patient that you made a report to CPS, consider the impact that this omission might have on your relationship with your patient. Consider a patient who knows a report was made to CPS but does not know who made the report. The patient may process their feelings about being reported with that professional, without knowing that it was this very person they are talking to who made the report. There are some considerable ethical concerns in this scenario.

Whether you decide to tell the patient or not, use your educational experience, expertise, and critical thinking skills to make this decision. Talk over your concerns with colleagues and supervisors. Role-play the conversation to become comfortable with what it might involve. The more you exercise these skills, the better they will serve you in the rest of your professional career.

Continuing Work with Patients after a Report: Addressing Risk through Professional Practice

You made a report to CPS, but you are still working with your patient. There are many things professional reporters can do, even after making a report to CPS, that can help protect children and support healthier family functioning. As a medical or healthcare professional, you are empowered through your role to support healthy family function and protect children by:

- Practicing your professional role to address children's and family's issues and concerns;
- Finding appropriate services or resources that the family needs to address a presenting problem,
- Making a referral for treatment for mental health concerns or substance use disorders,
- Providing a sounding board for the parents to inform their problem solving,
- Listening to the frustrations of a parent who doesn't know what to do to make a situation better, and/or
- Many other options, depending on the specific presenting circumstance.

A report to CPS is often not the end of a professional relationship with a patient, especially for some medical and healthcare professionals. If you adequately develop your professional relationship with your patient through the use of informed consent processes and gaining mutual trust, you may be even more important to your patient after making a report than before.

Protecting Patient Confidentiality Even When You Made a Report to CPS

The responsibility to protect patient confidentiality while simultaneously adhering to the legal responsibility of reporting suspicions of maltreatment is an obvious ethical conflict. While it is clear that professional standards of conduct accept AND expect medical and healthcare professionals to breach patient confidentiality to report appropriate suspicions of child maltreatment, professionals have another ethical obligation to minimize harm to a patient from this kind of disclosure. When communicating with CPS, professional reporters should provide the least amount of confidential patient information necessary to fulfill their legal and ethical obligations as reporters.

Even while making a report to CPS, you should protect your patient's confidentiality as much as possible. When making a report to CPS, you do not need to provide a complete assessment of your patient. Instead, you should provide the information necessary for fulfilling your legal obligation to report, as well as your ethical obligation to the larger society, while protecting as much of your patient's privacy as you can. Relevant ethical codes for medical and healthcare professionals make it clear that if you are sharing confidential information, whether with patient permission or based on other obligations that are ethically permissible, you should disclose the LEAST amount of confidential information necessary to achieve the desired purpose.

This means that if you decide to make a report to CPS, you are likely sharing confidential information required to make the report, but don't just give over ALL your confidential information on a patient. Make sure you are only providing information that is being asked for, and that the reason for the information is appropriate. Only provide information that is necessary for the CPS investigation. If CPS asks questions that you don't think are relevant to the case, you are not required to share the information. You can say no. As professionals governed by professional standards for ethical behavior, medical and healthcare professionals should feel empowered to push back against other professionals, like lawyers and caseworkers, who might not share the same ethical code or patient interests. If CPS wants information that you think is outside what is relevant to the report, CPS can seek a court order from a judge that would require you to provide more information.

The one caveat is when a patient, themselves, is asking the medical or healthcare professional to disclose confidential information to CPS.

When a patient releases the professional from the responsibility for patient confidentiality, they are exercising their right to autonomy. You can counsel your patient on their rights related to the release of confidential information, but, ultimately, you should abide by their wishes when provided with a written release.

Supporting Our Patients After a Report is Made

Whether we are the source of a report to CPS or working with a family who is reported by another source, medical and healthcare professionals can support patients after a report is made. We can serve as an advocate for a patient, if they would like us to be, even if we made the report to CPS. As a patient advocate, we can participate in case conferences and help clarify communication between our patients and CPS.

Test Questions

You made a report to CPS and have concerns for the impact on the family. Which of the following options is NOT one to consider?

a. Make contact with the CPS caseworker and explain your concerns for the impact on the family.
b. Instruct the family to prepare their children for interviews with CPS by telling them what to say.
c. Assist the family to find resources to support them through the CPS process.
d. Talk to your supervisor about your concerns.
e. Talk to your colleagues about your concerns.

You have decided to make a report to CPS about a particular family you work with, but you're concerned that the family will get angry with you for making the report. To manage your concerns you should:

a. Consult with your supervisor/colleagues to make a plan to address your concerns.
b. Tell the family that someone else made the report.
c. Make the report anonymously.
d. Terminate your professional relationship with the family.
e. Lie about your name when you make the report.

Once you have determined that you have the requisite level of suspicion to require a report in your state, you should:

a. Call CPS immediately.
b. Prepare for a call to CPS by gathering notes and information on the family.
c. Make sure your progress notes are up to date in the patient's file.
d. Make sure you get your supervisor's permission to report.
e. Call the police.

You made a report to CPS, and now they are asking you to provide copies of your patient's records. Which of the following is the most appropriate response to such a request?

a. Provide CPS with a copy of the patient's complete case file.
b. Insist that they have the patient sign a written release before providing any material to CPS.
c. Only provide CPS with a copy of material from the patient's case file that you deem as relevant to the information you provided in your report to CPS and/or necessary for the investigation.
d. Refuse to provide any material to CPS until they get an order from a judge.
e. Ask them to prepare a subpoena to support their request.

Which of the following is a way professionals can support a patient after making a report to CPS?

a. Serving as an advocate during communications between the patient and CPS.

b. Providing relevant materials to CPS when our patient provides a written release to do so.

c. Continuing to provide the patient with high-quality services to mitigate future harm.

d. Providing a referral to a service provider who can help the patient with a relevant presenting concern.

e. All of the answers are appropriate ways to support a patient after making a report to CPS.

Discussion Questions

- What is your level of comfort with telling your patient that you are making a report to CPS before or after making the call? What concerns do you have? What can you do to mitigate those concerns? Role-playing this scenario is recommended.
- You make a report to CPS, and the CPS worker asks you for a copy of your patient's case record. How do you respond? What are your concerns?

Resources & References

List of CPS hotline numbers in each state:

https://www.childwelfare.gov/organizations/?CWIGFunctionsaction=rols:main.dspList&rolType=Custom&RS_ID=5

Video example of CPS hotline call:

https://www.youtube.com/watch?v=gIVzg3ZDwuI

Lau, K.J., Krase, K.S. & Morse, R. (2008). Mandated reporting of child abuse and neglect: A practical guide for social workers. New York: Springer.

Child Welfare Information Gateway. (2020). Differential response: A primer for child welfare professionals. Washington, DC: U.S. Department of Health and Human Services, Children's Bureau. https://www.childwelfare.gov/pubPDFs/differential_response.pdf

8

Making an Impact Beyond Our Role as Reporters

Many professional reporters of suspected child maltreatment see their role as one outside of the child protection system. If we don't really have control over the circumstances that lead to our concerns for children's safety and if we don't work for CPS, we aren't responsible for what happens after we make a report, right? Wrong.

Professional reporters have a lot more influence in the lives of children and their families than we give ourselves credit for. We have influence as professionals who work with children and their families, as well as members of communities and society at large. There is a lot we can do in our personal and professional roles to work for improvements to systems that serve children and families, including CPS.

Micro Level Change

The focus of this book is preparing you as a professional reporter at the "micro," or individual, level. Throughout the last seven chapters we have explored how professionals can frame, reflect on, and act upon our reporter role, as well as your role as a medical or healthcare professional, in an effort to improve outcomes for children and families. However, there are other system levels that we can impact beyond the micro level, i.e., the mezzo and macro levels.

Mezzo Level Change

The micro level focuses on individuals, and the mezzo level focuses on the interaction of those individuals. The mezzo level includes families, groups, and organizations. As we consider our role as professional reporters of suspected child maltreatment, we should reflect on how we can navigate our role to support or enhance families, groups, and organizations.

Impact on Families

When we work with individuals, it is important to remember that they are a part of a family unit. Our work with an individual can impact the family at large as well. When we seek to protect an individual child, we might think of a parent negatively as a potential perpetrator or negligent caretaker. We need to remember that the parent is part of that child's family and that the parent was once a child themselves. When we can conceptualize that a child's protection is often synonymous with helping or supporting a family, we can make a larger positive impact whether we make a report to CPS or not.

To find out more about how parents and families experience CPS intervention, explore the publications of *Rise Magazine* (www.risemagazine.org). *Rise* is a New York City based non-profit that focuses on two goals:

1) To prevent unnecessary CPS involvement, and

2) To reform child welfare policy and practice so that families involved with CPS are less likely to be separated and more likely to reunify if children are removed.

Improving Organizational Policy and Practice

Many professional reporters conduct their practice in the context of a hospital system, agency or organization. Hospital systems, agencies and organizations that employ a significant number of mandated reporters usually have policies to guide the practice of reporting suspicions to CPS. Now that you have read this book, you should be ready to review such policies with a more informed perspective. Take some time to evaluate relevant agency policy and review agency practices. Consider the impact of CPS reporting on your organization's relationship with patients and the community you service. Are there any questions or concerns that should be explored?

Pay particular attention to how policies and practices might differentially impact patients who are economically disadvantaged. Also consider the experiences of patients who identify as BIPOC (Black, Indigenous, and People of Color). It may be time, for instance, for your agency to infuse implicit bias awareness into staff training efforts.

Macro Level Change

The macro level focuses on the impact of systems of a larger size. Opportunities for macro level intervention include policy at the community, local, state, federal, and national levels. There are a wide variety of reforms that have been proposed for changes to CPS policy, in particular. This spectrum of change ranges from simple updates to policies, like improving training for mandated reporters to the complete dismantling and replacement of the child protection system as a whole.

Training for Mandated Reporters

Researchers, policy makers, and professional reporters, themselves, have consistently called for increased and improved preparation of mandated reporters, including training initiatives. Some states require training for certain mandated reporters, but most mandated reporters do not get trained in their role. Specifically for medical and healthcare professionals, some states require training once in a lifetime in order to receive a license. Some states may include mandated reporter training in their continuing education programs for licensed professionals. Professionals who work in the school system may be required by state law to complete training annually in some states.

Research on mandated reporting is clear that professional reporters feel that they need more training and better training in order to adequately meet their legal requirements and best serve their patients. Consider your own experiences that have prepared you for your role as a mandated reporter. What helped you understand your role? What could be better? And what can you do to improve your own preparation for this role, as well as to support a better system to prepare others in this role?

Ensuring Social and Racial Justice in the Child Protection System

As individual reporters, we can ensure social and racial justice in our own practice through improving our awareness and working to eliminate the influence of our own biases on our decision making. At the macro level, professional reporters should demand examination of systems (like educational, medical, and mental health systems) that lend to inequities in CPS by income and race and take action to challenge and ultimately change these systems. Alternatively, or in addition to, we can press for the expansion of "differential response" programs, which replace traditional CPS practices with models based on mental and behavioral health practice including engagement, assessment, and responsive intervention.

Calls for Elimination and Abolition

As recognition of the problems inherent in the current CPS system grows, there is increasing demand for overhauling mandated reporting requirements and eliminating the child protection system, at least in its current form. Central to calls for dismantling mandated reporting and/or dissolving CPS are concerns for social and racial justice or, more generally, the belief that CPS, as currently designed, is ineffectual. There is also growing concern that mandated reporting, in particular, infringes on the autonomy of professional reporters and that professionals might be more effective at prevention or intervention efforts, if not for broadly defined legally proscribed CPS reporting requirements.

The Ultimate Goals: Protecting Children and Supporting Families

Ultimately, we all want our work to protect children and support families. We can't do it alone. We need policy at the local, state, federal, and international levels to make children and families a priority. Medical and healthcare professionals need to use individual and collective voices to demand policies that would reduce need for CPS intervention.

Imagine what would happen if our society prioritized child care, income, and food security. How great would it be if all working parents could take a day off from work when their child was sick, without fear of losing a day's pay or their job? Or perhaps society could support a system where everyone could afford to eat, regardless of the quality of their job? You know, like ensuring a living wage. Okay. Maybe I'm getting off topic or being a little too political for your taste. But, I think you get my point. If medical and healthcare professionals truly care about kids, you have to care about their parents and families, too.

How do we get all this done? First, talk to your colleagues, family, and friends, and explain how preventing child maltreatment isn't just less expensive than treating or responding to it, it is the moral and righteous thing to do. Then, we need to elect policymakers who make these concerns a priority. Call or email your policymakers. Heck, even tweet them. Make your voices heard until policymakers don't just acknowledge the concerns that we have, but they actually move forward on our calls for action.

Discussion Questions

- What are you willing to do in order to make change in the child protection system at the micro, mezzo, and macro levels?
- What social issues do you think are most important to address in order to protect children from maltreatment?

Kathryn Suzanne Krase, Ph.D., J.D., M.S.W., is the Principal Consultant for Krase Consulting, in Brooklyn, New York. Dr. Krase also leads the initiative, Making the Tough Call, a project that aims to educates professional reporters of suspected child maltreatment so that they are prepared to intervene to protect children when necessary, while respecting and supporting family integrity wherever possible.

For more information about Dr. Krase, visit: https://www.kraseconsulting.com

For more information about Making the Tough Call, visit:

https://www.makingthetoughcall.info

If you would like to contact Dr. Krase to discuss training opportunities, or related consultation services, email her at: Kathryn@KraseConsulting.com

www.ingramcontent.com/pod-product-compliance
Lightning Source LLC
Chambersburg PA
CBHW070833160726
48004CB00001B/363